Cross Training

Cross Training

How to Live the Jesus-Life

Jonathan Jones II

ISBN-13: 978-1706416012

Printed in the United States of America.

First Edition, 2019

Cover image: Fachry Zella Devandra on Unsplash.com
Cover design: Jonathan Jones II

To disciple-makers everywhere
who share the joyful good news of Jesus.

Cross Training
INTRODUCTION

Jesus gave his followers the mission of relationally making disciples. Being a disciple of Jesus is more than a belief system—it is a lifestyle. But how can believers help others to become genuine disciples of Christ? *Cross Training* provides a roadmap for guiding someone into "the Jesus-life." There are three sections to this book.

Part 1: Begin is a survey of the Bible's grand, unifying narrative and guides the reader into finding their place in God's big story. Each of these six sessions are intended to be conversation starters between two or three friends. By exploring God's sweeping plan for humanity, you will be challenged to consider seriously becoming a follower of Jesus.

In **Part 2: Basic,** the training continues by laying the foundational principles of the discipled life with material intended to initiate accelerated spiritual growth. These thirteen session are designed as content for a weekly discipleship group meeting. Once completed, the material can then be used to replicate the process.

Finally, in **Part 3: Beyond**, the new follower of Christ is guided into forming a new habit of daily discipleship with forty days of discipleship meditations. These devotional guides (for six weeks) reinforce one's commitment to daily follow Jesus.

Disciple-makers are encouraged to begin with the appendix. There you will find helpful tips and advice on how to share your faith and start your own discipleship group.

CONTENTS

Part 1: BEGIN
Finding Your Place in God's Story

Part 2: BASIC
Foundations of Discipleship

Part 3: BEYOND
Forty Days of Daily Discipleship

Welcome to BEGIN:
Finding Your Place in God's Story

Everyone loves a good story. Stories are powerful. They possess the capability to heal, restore, and inspire. Human history is framed by stories. From cave drawings, to oral tradition, folklore, myths, legends, and blockbuster movies, we have always been captivated by the power of storytelling. From the bedtime stories of our youth to the captivating yarn-weavers of old age, we are drawn in by stories. And the stories that move us the most are the ones that are *true*.

Everybody has a Story

All of us have stories to tell. Each of us have faced challenges and have overcome obstacles. The human experience is enriched when we share our stories with each other. Every living person is in the midst of writing their story. Each moment is a new sentence, every day is a new chapter. All of us want to have meaningful stories to tell, lives that are rich and significant.

In his book, *A Million Miles in a Thousand Years: How I Learned to Live a Better Story*, Donald Miller discusses how many people end up giving up on their stories. We launch into adulthood with high aspirations of changing the world, finding adventure, and carefully crafting a monumental life. But we get into the middle of life and discover that it is much harder than we thought. As Miller writes, *"They can't see the distant shore anymore, and they wonder if their paddling is moving them forward. None of the trees behind them are getting smaller and none of the trees ahead are getting bigger. They take it out on their spouses, and they go looking for an easier story."* Even now, you may feel like your story is not what you hoped, like there is an exciting drama out there but you are stuck in the commercial break.

But remarkable things happen in your life when you start to find a good storyline to follow. As Miller later writes, *"And once you live a good story, you get a taste for a kind of meaning in life and you can't go back to being normal; you can't go back to meaningless scenes stitched together by the forgettable thread of wasted time."* So the key is finding a good narrative to follow. Perhaps somewhere there is an author who has written a compelling story.

Finding God?

In 1961, the first human to journey into outer space was the Russian cosmonaut Yurl Gagarin. Upon his return, the Soviet leader Khrushchev boldly declared that humans returned from outer space and God was not there. In response, the Christian apologist C.S. Lewis wrote an essay in 1963 called "The Seeing Eye." There he made a profound observation. Lewis said that looking for God in space is like trying to find Shakespeare in one of his plays. More to the point, it would be akin to Hamlet climbing into the attic of his castle trying to find Shakespeare.[1] If the God described in the Bible exists, he would not be like a man in the attic. Rather he would be the Playwright. He would be the grand storyteller writing the "Big Story" of all existence.

God has a Story

Evidence all around us points to God. Francis Collins came to see this evidence clearly. Collins was the geneticist who led the Human Genome Project (begun in 1990 and completed in 2003) responsible for mapping the human DNA. In 2006, following this project, he published the book *The Language of God: A Scientist Presents Evidence for Belief.* In the book he states, *"Think of DNA as an instructional script, a software program, sitting in the nucleus of the cell."*[2] If there is a software program, there must be a programmer. Or returning to the story metaphor, God is the Author, the world is his story, and we are his characters.

But the idea of an all-powerful being can be greatly intimidating. Are we simply pawns on God's chessboard? Are we little trifles made for his amusement? Did he simply write the story and step away? Did he just leave us here to be players on the stage? In the words of Shakespeare's *Macbeth*, is life simply a "tale (story) told by an idiot" that signifies nothing?

In the Bible, John the Apostle's "favorite designation of Jesus" is, "the sent One."[3] Jesus is the one who "comes from above" and is "above all" (John 3:31). He is the Creator and the one who wrote the story of life itself—*"All things were made through him, and without him was not anything made that was made"* (John 1:3). But more than simply being the Author of Life (Acts 3:15), our Creator descended into his Creation (John 3:13).

This reality is vividly illustrated by author Timothy Keller when he points to the life of the British novelist Dorothy Sayers. One of the first women to be granted a degree from Oxford, Sayers wrote a dozen mystery novels between the two World Wars. Her novels tell of an amateur sleuth named Peter Wimsey, an eccentric fellow, very flawed and not easy to get along with. Along the way, Sayers introduces Harriet Vane (a mystery writer educated at Oxford). Harriet Vane and Peter Wimsey have a budding romance and finally marry. Wimsey's troubled life is finally rescued by Harriet Vane. Many literary critics believe the fictional Harriet Vane is really Dorothy Sayers herself. It seems that the author fell in love with the character she wrote and then inserted herself into the story to save him.[4] That is exactly what God did for us. He created us, loved us, and wrote himself into the story of life (in Jesus) to rescue us. He did not come to simply provide a way for us to rescue ourselves...he came, himself, to rescue us.

The "Big Story" of Existence

The Bible is filled with lots of little stories. For those new to the

Bible, it can be overwhelming and intimidating. What do all these little stories mean? When you look more closely, you will find that all these little stories are woven together into a grand saga. All of the "lower stories" are designed to tell a much larger "Upper Story," the big story of our existence.[5] When you understand the main story of the Bible, all the little stories fit into place. That is how God's Story, in the Bible, is presented.

Our lives follow the same pattern. There are many things that happen to us that don't seem to make sense. We struggle to understand the monotony and seeming randomness of our daily lives. We need some means of framing our "lower stories." We need an "Upper Story" that will help us make sense of it all. It is easy to be inundated and overwhelmed with the flood of information available today. But facts alone don't give meaning. It takes *a story* to provide a framework, a context, by which to understand the facts.[6] The Bible provides a grand framework that helps you understand your place in God's story.

How to Use this Study Guide

Cross Training, Part 1: BEGIN is designed to help you understand your purpose in God's story. This first section is comprised of 6 sessions (with challenge assignments) to help you see the main storyline of Scripture and how your life fits into this framework. There are also homework exercises between each session. This material works best as simply a conversation between two friends. If you choose to use it with a group, it is best to keep it limited to 3-5 people. Keeping the group small provides opportunity for more interaction, which is crucial for this study.

This material is designed for those who are open to considering the Christian life. For those highly skeptical and want to dig deeper into the claims of Christianity, I highly recommend *The Reason for God: Belief in the Age of Skepticism* (New York: Riverhead, 2008) by Timothy Keller.

Ready to hear a good story? Best yet, this story is true. It is the grandest story ever told, the very story of your existence and why you are here. It's time to find your place in God's story.

"God invites us to come as we are, not to stay as we are."
(Timothy Keller)

Part 1: Begin

Finding Your Place in God's Story

1

Our First Meeting

Sharing Our Stories

This Bible study is designed to be a faith sharing experience. These studies are intended to explore what the Bible says about having a deep and intimate relationship with God. These lessons work best when two or three friends get together with the desire to grow together in relationship with God. In your first meeting together, try and get to know each other better on a spiritual level.

Sharing Our Spiritual Journeys

1. Discuss your spiritual journeys with one another.

2. What is your experience with God and religion?

3. What is the most difficult thing you have experienced in life? How did you get through it?

4. In your life right now, do you feel close to God or do you feel like he is far away? Explain.

5. How would you describe your relationship with God right now? [7]

    - In the street looking at God's house

    - Walking up the sidewalk

    - Knocking on his front door

    - Sitting in the living room as part of the family

6. Alternative Question: How would you describe your relationship with God at this point? [8]

    - Strangers

    - Acquaintances

    - Dating

    - Engaged

    - Happily married

    - Unhappily married

    - Separated

    - Divorced

    - Something in between

Getting to Know God

1. **Read Acts 17:22-23.** How would you describe the *religion* of the people of Athens? What was their personal knowledge of God?

2. **Read Acts 17:24-28.** Is God approachable? Is God far away in some distant galaxy?

3. **Read 2 Kings 6:15-17.** How might we be blinded to the presence of God today?

4. **Read Deuteronomy 4:29.** Is it possible to "find God" today? Based on this verse, how can this be done?

Your Soul-Work Challenge For this Week[9]
Spiritual Self-Reflection

1. List, in order of importance and time priority, five goals you are seeking to reach in your lifetime:

   (1) _____

   _____

   (2) _____

   _____

   (3) _____

   _____

   (4) _____

   _____

   (5) _____

   _____

2. Write a brief autobiography of your spiritual life to date:

3. What is a specific personal struggle that you are trying to overcome?

4. List your five deepest convictions. These are things you believe most deeply and most impact your life.

(1) _____

(2) _____

(3) _____

(4) _____

(5) _____

This Week's Gospel Story Reading:

Read the **Gospel of John chapters 1-4** this week. Take note of the following questions:

1. What do you learn about Jesus?

2. What do you learn about people/yourself?

3. How will you obey this passage this week?

Notes:

2

Our Second Meeting

The Beginning of the Story

Where Our Story Begins (Genesis 1-2)

The beginning of life as we know it all starts in Genesis 1. This chapter describes a powerful God who creates the heavens and the earth and then fills that environment with life. But the creation of the Universe is only the subplot of this grand story. The real point is that God wants to be *with you*. God admires the beauty of his creative work by saying six times "It is good" (Genesis 1:3,10,12,18,21,25). But all of this beautiful environment is just a display case for his real work of art.[10] God's crowning achievement would be the human race. He created humans in his own image and likeness (Genesis 1:26-27). When he creates the first man and first woman, he steps back and says "It is *very* good" (Genesis 1:31). The Grand Canyon, Mount Everest, the Sahara, rain forests…none of these are as beautiful in God's eyes as you. His desire was to create human children that he could enjoy, love, and embrace into the divine community. God is the first parent. He brought you into the world for his pleasure, and even now he longs to be with you.

1. **Read Genesis 1:27.** What does it mean when someone says to a parent that his child is their "spitting image?"

2. **Read Psalm 139:13-16.** How does it make you feel to know God thinks you are "wonderfully made?"

3. **Read Psalm 8.** How does it make you feel to know God has "crowned you with glory and honor?"

4. **Read Zephaniah 3:17.** How does this verse describe God's joy over you?

The Divine Community (Genesis 1:26)

The Bible consistently teaches that there is only one God. Yet, this one God exists in community. This seems to be a contradiction to us. It is as if we are one-dimensional begins trying to understand a three-dimensional God. God exists in a community of love: Father, Son, and Spirit. This divine community exists in love and joyfulness. Father, Son and Spirit commune with, exalt, glorify, and defer to one another. God created us, his human children, to enter into this community of divine love. God wants you to be in his family.

5. **Read Genesis 1:26.** What do you think might be the significance of the word "us" in this verse?

6. **Read Genesis 1:2.** Who was present with God the Father at Creation?

7. **Read John 1:1-14.** Who else was present and united with God the Father from the start?

8. **Read John 17:20-26.** What does God want us to enjoy with him?

Your Soul-Work Challenge For this Week
Becoming Aware of God's Presence

1. Write out a short and honest prayer to God letting him hear your heart and asking him to help you to discover a deep, *personal* relationship with him:

    My Father in Heaven,

2. In **Psalm 46:10** God says, *"Be still and know that I am God."* To experience the goodness of God, we must slow down, become quiet, and learn to be aware of his beauty around us.[11]

    This week, find 5 minutes each day to sit in silence. Try and quiet your mind and focus upon the beauty of God's created world. Think of God as a great artist and you are his art student; pay close attention to the detail of his artwork. By looking to God's creation, we can become more aware of his power and presence.

This Week's Gospel Story Reading:

Read the **Gospel of John chapters 5-8** this week. Take note of anything that jumps out at you.

1. What do you learn about Jesus?

2. What do you learn about people/yourself?

3. How will you obey this passage this week?

Notes:

3

Our Third Meeting

The Conflict in the Story

What Happened to the World? (Genesis 3)

God did not just want a good life for his children; he wanted a perfect life for them. He created a paradise-home for his offspring. There was plenty of food and water, yet no pain, no death, no disease. And best of all, God lived among them there in the garden (Genesis 3:8). This place was heaven on earth. But that is not the kind of world we live in today. *So what happened?* God not only loved his human children enough to give them a perfect home; he loved them enough to give them freedom of choice. Every parent's greatest desire is that their children will love them. God gave us the ability to choose relationship with him or to live independent from him. Adam and Eve chose independence from God. But people were designed to reflect God's image. Humans choosing to live apart from God are like fish choosing to live on dry land. Such is contrary to our design. When this happened, the mirror shattered and the perfect paradise became corrupted.

1. **Read Genesis 2:15-17.** How was the gift of freedom of choice presented to humanity?

2. **Read Genesis 3.** What were the consequences of Adam and Eve's sin? To Adam? To Eve? To the serpent? To the world?

3. **Read Romans 5:12-14.** What was the lasting result of Adam and Eve's sin?

4. **Read Genesis 8:20-22.** What lasting effects are rooted in the human heart as a result of Adam and Eve's sin?

The "Double Trouble" for Us All [12]

Adam and Eve chose separation from God, and God honored that choice. God's nature is truth and integrity, and he cannot go back on his word. Spiritual death (separation from God) was the consequence of humanity's sin. But like any loving parent, God's desire is that his wayward children would desire to return to him. So from the beginning, God created a road for relationship with him to be restored. God would eventually provide a hero that would pay the price (be bruised) for humanity's sin, while he would crush the head of humanity's tempter (Genesis 3:15). This hero is needed because sin creates a legal problem with God. We are guilty of rebellion against him. Therefore, we need forgiveness of our past sins. This is the first part of our trouble.

But we don't just need our records cleared; we need spiritual rehabilitation. God desires your love. Like a parent longing for a wayward child, God wants you to come back home (cf. Luke 15:20-24).

This requires not only forgiveness, but a change of heart. Our hearts have become contaminated with the desire for sinful things. Our hearts are sick. We need a spiritual heart transplant. This is the second part of our trouble.

(In our next two meetings, we will take a closer look at each of these two problems.)

5. **Read Isaiah 59:1-2.** What separates us from a real relationship with God?

6. **Read Leviticus 17:11.** What is needed for forgiveness of sins (atonement) to be made possible?

7. In his book *Counterfeit Gods*, Timothy Keller wrote: *"...God's grace and forgiveness, while free to the recipient, are always costly for the giver.... From the earliest parts of the Bible, it was understood that God could not forgive without sacrifice. No one who is seriously wronged can "just forgive" the perpetrator.... But when you forgive, that means you absorb the loss and the debt. You bear it yourself. All forgiveness, then, is costly."* [13]

Has there been a time in your life when forgiving someone cost you something?

8. **Read John 3:16-17.** What does this verse say to you about how much God was willing to sacrifice to provide your forgiveness?

9. **Read Hosea 11:1-9.** What insight do these verses give you about God's desire for his human children to return to him?

Your Soul-Work Challenge For this Week[14]
Getting Real About Yourself

1. **Read Psalm 32:1-5.** According to these verses, what is required in order to find forgiveness and spiritual healing?

2. **Read Galatians 5:19-21.** Below is a list of the types of behaviors that harm our relationship with God and life in his kingdom. Read over this list and consider times when you may have been guilty of these behaviors.

SEXUAL IMMORALITY (Greek: *porneia*): Any sexual sin. Includes adultery (sexual intercourse involving people one or both of whom are married, but not to each other), fornication (sexual activity between unmarried people), homosexuality (Romans 1:26-27), prostitution (1 Corinthians 6:15-20), sex with relatives (Leviticus 18:6), sex with animals (Leviticus 18:23), etc.

IMPURITY (Greek: *akatharsia*): Unclean thoughts and behavior, especially sexual in nature. Sinful thinking, anything vulgar, wrong thoughts, lust, wrong motives, use of pornography, impure sexual fantasy.

DEBAUCHERY ("lustful pleasures"-NLT) (Greek: *aselgia*): Living with no self-control and rebelling against all moral rules; doing anything you desire by ignoring right moral conduct (especially with regard to sexual desire). An eagerness to indulge in any pleasure God has said is wrong; sexually unrestrained and promiscuous. Includes sexually suggestive dancing, immodest dress and speech. It also includes sexually touching someone to whom you are not married (cf. Ezekiel 23:3).

IDOLATRY (Greek: *eidololatria*): Putting anything before God. Giving or devoting your time, substance, talents or self to anything that keeps you from obeying and following God in every way. Anything can become an idol in your life: status symbols, investments, pleasure and wants. Even innocent things can becoming an all-consuming idol in your life such as: engrossing sports or hobbies, selfish ambitions, relationships, property, possessions, school, work, pride, job addiction, etc.

WITCHCRAFT ("sorcery" –NLT) (Greek: *pharmakeia*): Especially refers to sorcery and magic and the occult. Idolatrous worship often involved the use of hallucinogenic drugs (the English word "pharmacy" comes from this Greek word); seeking spiritual guidance from sources other than God. Includes astrology (the stars are in control of your fate, and so God does not rule), putting faith in horoscopes, Satan worship, the occult, magic spells, good luck charms or pictures, praying to saints, reading tarot cards, palm reading, channeling, etc. (see Deuteronomy 18:9-12).

HATRED ("hostility" –NLT) (Greek: *echthra*): Feelings of hostility, hatred, animosity and ill-will toward others; to have hostile feelings and actions toward another person. Wishing ill or harm on anyone. Looking down on anyone, bitter feelings, wanting revenge and resentment. Hating someone in your heart is spiritual murder (see Matthew 5:21-22).

DISCORD ("quarreling" –NLT; "strife" –ESV) (Greek: *eris*): Engaging in rivalry with positions being taken. Involvement in disagreements that destroy relationships; having an attitude of being contentious with people. Anything which breaks up relationships. Stirring up trouble, an inability to get along with people, arguing, gossip, malicious talk and criticalness of others. God hates people who cause division (Proverbs 6:16-19).

JEALOUSY (Greek: *zelos*): Used in a negative sense here as having intense bad feelings about the achievements of other people. Possessiveness over others. Not sharing. Wanting something that someone else has.

FITS OF RAGE ("outbursts of anger" –NLT) (Greek: *thumos*): Intense feelings of displeasure with anger getting out of control. Uncontrolled anger, losing your temper, temper tantrums, quick temper, angry shouting, cussing and profanity, fighting.

SELFISH AMBITION ("rivalries" –ESV) (Greek: *eritheia*): Seeking to "get ahead" at any cost. Living to please yourself. Wanting one's own way; an overly competitive spirit. Not willing to do menial or demeaning tasks, refusing to admit to being wrong, arrogance, doing things for honor or glory, wanting to look good for others, refusing to compromise, pride, selfishness and independence.

DISSENSIONS (Greek: *dichostasia*): Causing divisions (similar to DISCORD above). Rebelling against authority. Not submitting. Habitually disagreeing with people, arguing, causing divisions, starting arguments, stirring up trouble.

FACTIONS ("divisions" –NLT) (Greek: *hairesis*): Group loyalty in the negative sense of being a part of a group that will not associate with others. Feeling superior to others. Cliques, refusing to associate with someone because they are different from you. Wanting to only be with your "own" kind; prejudice, bigotry and racism.

ENVY (Greek: *phthonos*): Desiring something another person has while wishing that they did not have it at all (such as wealth, position, status, recognition, ability, physical features, spirituality, relationships, possessions, etc.).

DRUNKENNESS (Greek: *methe*): Overindulging in alcohol and becoming intoxicated with strong drink. In general might apply to anything which causes one to lose control ("drunk with power," etc.). Intoxication, alcohol, drug abuse. Using anything to replace God as the comfort and help in your life. Scripture repeatedly warned about the dangers of alcohol abuse and the sin of drunkenness and addiction (Proverbs 20:1; 23:31-35).

ORGIES ("wild parties" –NLT; "carousing" –NASB) (Greek: *komos*): Literally "excessive feasting." Strong drink and reclining at the table at ancient feasts would often lead to unrestrained group sex. Living without restraint. Includes "partying" and sexual parties, unrestrained sex, vandalism, carousing. Modern applications include keg parties, drinking games, sexual orgies, spouse swapping, etc.

AND THE LIKE: Lying, stealing, cheating, deceit, etc. This does not claim to be a complete list of sins. Other "sin lists" in the New Testament include: Romans 1:18-32; 1 Corinthians 5:9-11; 6:9-11; Ephesians 4:25-5:7; Colossians 3:5-10; 2 Timothy 3:1-5; Revelation 21:8; 22:15.

3. After reviewing the "sin list" from Galatians above, try to remember **ANYTIME** in your life that you have been guilty of these sins. Confess those sins to God by writing them down, giving specific examples so that the light of God's presence can destroy the darkness. *If it comes to mind, it is worth writing down.*

4. **Read James 5:16.** How does this verse say that we can experience spiritual healing from our sins?

This Week's Gospel Story Reading:

Read the **Gospel of John chapters 9-12** this week. Take note of anything that jumps out at you.

1. What do you learn about Jesus?

2. What do you learn about people/yourself?

3. How will you obey this passage this week?

4

Our Fourth Meeting

The Hero of the Story

The Great Reversal of Grace (Ephesians 2)

When we get real about ourselves and our personal sin, the guilt and regret can be overwhelming. We often make many attempts at trying to "redeem" ourselves. We frequently are deceived into thinking that doing good works, engaging in religious rituals, or trying to be good morally will right the wrongs of the past. Yet, all of us have the haunting feeling that our guilt remains. How can we be certain that our past is really forgiven by God? We can do nothing to save ourselves; we need a Savior. We need the grace of God. Sin deserves the payment of a penalty. But if the penalty is paid, we can experience freedom. By placing our faith in a Savior (Jesus Christ), we get the opposite of what we deserve. That is because Jesus traded places with us. This is the great reversal of grace. By accepting Jesus in faith, Jesus trades places with us, and we get the opposite of what we deserve.

1. **Read Ephesians 2:1-10.** How do we receive the saving grace of God? How do we *not* receive it? What is the difference?

2. **Read Matthew 27:24-54.** At Jesus' death, he cries out with a "loud voice." Jesus was being cast out of God's presence so that you could enter (Psalm 22; 2 Corinthians 5:21). Traditionally, the events around Jesus' death are called his "passion." This is a Latin word that means suffering. Yet, we often use the word passion to describe deep love. Deep love often involves deep suffering. We are Jesus' passion—his love that was worth dying for.[15] How does that make you feel?

3. **Read 1 Peter 2:21-25.** How does it make you feel to know that God (in Jesus) is willing to "absorb" your debt and bear it himself?

4. **Read Isaiah 49:14-16 and John 20:24-29.** What do these verses say to you about God's love for you?

5. **Read 2 Corinthians 5:17-21.** Jesus not only traded *places* with you, he traded *faces* with you.[16] For the believer, God looks at *Jesus* and sees the believer's sin. What, then, does God see when he looks at the believer?

New Life and Christ's Death (Romans 6:1-14)

In the great reversal of grace, Jesus trades places with us. Jesus *lived to die.* We must *die to live.* In Jesus's death, *he* receives our penalty. But as believers, we receive Jesus' perfect relationship with the Father in Heaven. This new life comes to us through Christ's death. We receive this new life when we join Jesus in his death. We must "die" to self, that we might live for God. The Bible makes clear that there is a *specific event* where we are "united with Christ in his death," and as a result we arise to have new life.

6. **Read Luke 9:23-26.** What do you think it means to "deny yourself" in order to follow Jesus?

7. **Read Galatians 2:20.** Spiritual life results when Christ comes to "live inside" you (cf. John 14:23). In order for this to happen, what must first occur?

8. **Read Romans 6:1-3.** *How* do we get "into" Jesus' death?

9. **Read Romans 6:4-5.** At what point does a believer enter "newness of life" and become "united" to Jesus Christ?

10. **Read Romans 6:6-14.** According to these verses, how can we be set free from sin?

Your Soul-Work Challenge For this Week
The Believer's Wedding Ceremony

1. **Read Romans 6:1-14 again slowly.** Meditate deeply on the meaning of these words. Now compare these words with the graphic[17] below:

the Gospel re-enacted in Baptism

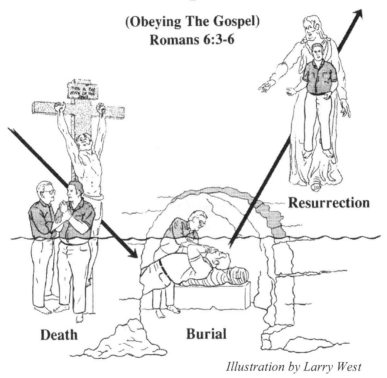

(Obeying The Gospel)
Romans 6:3-6

Resurrection

Death   **Burial**

Illustration by Larry West

2. Have you ever been baptized into Christ? If yes, what were the circumstances of your baptism? (How old were you? How were you baptized? For what reason were you baptized?)

3. **Read Ephesians 5:25-33.** What illustration is used here to describe the seriousness of being united to Christ?

4. **Read Luke 14:25-31.** What do these verses say to you about the seriousness of committing to follow Christ?

This Week's Gospel Story Reading:

Read the **Gospel of John chapters 13-17** this week. Take note of anything that jumps out at you.

1. What do you learn about Jesus?

2. What do you learn about people/yourself?

3. How will you obey this passage this week?

Biblical Evidence on Christian Baptism

This is not a complete list. Feel free to add to the list from your study of the Bible. However, please pay careful attention to what these verses are clearly teaching on the topic.

Biblical Statement (*Passages are taken from the English Standard Version. Feel free to compare other translations*).	What does this verse say occurs at baptism?
Acts 2:38 "And Peter said to them, 'Repent and be baptized every one of you in the name of Jesus Christ for the forgiveness of your sins, and you will receive the gift of the Holy Spirit.'"	
Acts 22:16 "And now why do you wait? Rise and be baptized and wash away your sins, calling on his name."	
Romans 6:3-4 "Do you not know that all of us who have been baptized into Christ Jesus were baptized into his death? We were buried therefore with him by baptism into death, in order that, just as Christ was raised from the dead by the glory of the Father, we too might walk in newness of life."	
1 Corinthians 12:13 "For in one Spirit we were all baptized into one body—Jews or Greeks, slaves or free—and all were made to drink of one Spirit."	

Galatians 3:27 "For as many of you as were baptized into Christ have put on Christ."	
Colossians 2:12 "…having been buried with him in baptism, in which you were also raised with him through faith in the powerful working of God, who raised him from the dead."	
1 Peter 3:21 "Baptism, which corresponds to this, now saves you, not as a removal of dirt from the body but as an appeal to God for a good conscience, through the resurrection of Jesus Christ."	
Mark 16:16 "And he said to them, 'Go into all the world and proclaim the gospel to the whole creation. Whoever believes and is baptized will be saved, but whoever does not believe will be condemned."	

5

Our Fifth Meeting

The Healing of the Story

The Indwelling of the Holy Spirit

God's desire is not simply to forgive us of our sins. He wants to heal our spirits. He wants to give us new lives. God desires to give us new hearts and transform our inner selves to once again reflect his image. God does this work himself by sending his Holy Spirit to reside within the believer's heart. The Holy Spirit brings spiritual renewal and healing to our brokenness.

1. **Read Ezekiel 36:26-27.** What type of spiritual surgery will God do upon the heart of a believer?

2. **Read Acts 2:36-39 and 1 Corinthians 12:12-13.** At what point are we given the gift of the Holy Spirit and drink from his blessings?

3. **Read Acts 19:1-7.** Is it possible for a person to be baptized for a wrong reason and not receive the Holy Spirit? What is the basis of receiving the Holy Spirit?

4. **Read John 4:7-14 and John 7:37-39.** What is the "living water" that Jesus provides that can quench our thirst for significance, satisfaction, and purpose in life?

The Spirit's Work is Character Transformation

The Holy Spirit always glorifies Jesus (John 16:14). The primary work of the Holy Spirit is to transform our characters to be more like Jesus. The Spirit does not do this automatically without our effort. Rather, the Spirit provides moral power to assist our desires to be more like Christ in our character.

5. **Read Galatians 4:6.** What "Spirit" does God send into the heart of baptized believers?

6. **Read Galatians 5:22-24.** What types of attitudes and behaviors are present where the Holy Spirit resides?

7. **Read Romans 8:1-11.** What is the difference between setting your mind on the things of the Spirit and setting your mind on the things of the flesh?

8. **Read 2 Corinthians 3:18.** From where does character transformation come?

9. **Read John 14:23 and Revelation 3:20.** Have you allowed God's presence inside of your heart?

Your Soul-Work Challenge For this Week
Healing from the Inside Out

1. One paraphrase of **Matthew 5:3** says, *"You're blessed when you're at the end of your rope. With less of you there is more of God and his rule"* (MSG). In what ways might there be blessing in brokenness?

2. **Read Psalm 34:18.** Spend time reflecting deeply upon these words.

3. Spend some time considering ways you feel spiritually broken. Go to a Christian friend (whom you trust) and share a specific area of spiritual need, sin, or area of repeated defeat in your life, and ask that person to pray for you.

4. **Read Psalm 51:1-12.** What does this passage say to you about spiritual brokenness and how you can be healed?

5. **Read Titus 3:3-7.** Spiritual renewal comes from the Holy Spirit. In what ways do you need to be *renewed* by Him?

This Week's Gospel Story Reading:

Read the **Gospel of John chapters 18-21** this week. Take note of anything that jumps out at you.

1. What do you learn about Jesus?

2. What do you learn about people/yourself?

3. How will you obey this passage this week?

Notes:

6

Our Sixth Meeting

The Life of the Story

Gathering with Other Believers

God never intended for you to be a *spiritual-lone-ranger*. The community of the faithful is called "the church" in Scripture. The word church simply means assembly. God does not intend for his church to be some cold, religious organization. His church is to be a dynamic, living organism. It is often called "the body" in the Bible. When you were baptized, you were automatically added to God's worldwide assembly of the saved (Acts 2:47; 1 Corinthians 12:13). This "one body" is the universal gathering of those who are "enrolled in heaven" (Hebrews 12:22-23). While God has added you to his family automatically, it is important that you find a place where disciples regularly meet and get involved in the work of God's kingdom at a local level (cf. Acts 9:26).

1. **Read Hebrews 12:22-29.** How is the assembly of God's people described in these verses? What kind of kingdom have you entered?

2. **Read Acts 2:37-47 and Acts 4:32-35.** What kind of community was formed by the followers of Jesus?

3. **Read 1 Corinthians 12:12-26.** Why do you think it is important for you to get personally involved in the work of "the body?"

4. **Read Hebrews 10:19-25.** Why is it important that you consistently assemble with other believers?

The Community of God Restored

Just like the angels, God created us to glorify him and give him praise (Isaiah 43:7). God's intention has always been that we would be in his family, embraced within the divine community. Followers of Christ have been adopted into God's family by the Spirit (Romans 8:15) and by faith in Jesus (Galatians 3:26) have been made citizens of the kingdom of heaven (Philippians 3:20). But while we live upon the earth, Christians are part of the assembly of God's people. We are the community of Christ. While we wait upon Jesus to return, we assemble together around the table to worship and remember him until he comes. We share the message of Jesus and live out his kingdom purpose on this earth.

5. **Read 1 Corinthians 10:16-17; 11:23-26.** When we assemble at the table for communion, with whom are we communing?

6. **Read Ephesians 2:13-22.** Through Christ, what has God built from the diversity of the human race?

7. **Read Matthew 6:9-13 (especially verse 10) and Luke 4:18-19.**
   How should disciples live in the world in order that God's will
   might be done on earth as it is in heaven?

8. **Read Revelation 21:1-4.** What is God's greatest desire for the
   community of his people?

Your Soul-Work Challenge For this Week
Are You Ready?

Choosing to follow Jesus is the most important commitment you can make in your life. It is a very serious and personal decision, not to be entered lightly. Your motivation for following Jesus is vitally important. You should not become a Christian because you are feeling pressured or manipulated. *It is a decision you must make when you are ready.* Jesus told his followers to "count the cost" before choosing to follow him (Luke 14:27-30). Jesus discouraged people from choosing to follow him too quickly if they were not willing to finish what they start (Luke 9:57-62). You need to know what you are getting into by following Jesus. However, none of us know what tomorrow holds or how many days of life we have left. Because life is brief, salvation is crucial, and eternity is never-ending, there should be a sense of urgency in following Jesus.

1. **Read James 4:13-17.** How is life described here?

2. **Read 2 Corinthians 6:1-2.** When is the "accepted time" for you to come to God in obedience and be united with Christ?

3. **Read Acts 8:26-40.** What was the timing of this Ethiopian's decision to follow Christ? Where did this happen? Who was present?

4. **Read Acts 22:1-16.** When Ananias spoke with Saul about becoming a Christian, what question did he ask (See verse 16)? How would you answer this question?

Deciding to follow Jesus is a very personal decision—one that you will make when you are ready. When that moment comes, your Christian friends will gladly assist you at any time, day or night.

Where Do I Go From Here?
Daily Quiet Time with God

Now that we have completed this study, where do you go from here? One of the most important things you can do as a disciple of Jesus is to make daily, quiet time with God a priority in your life. This time is spent in prayer, reading, reflection, introspection and meditation. Being a disciple of Jesus is a daily choice requiring intentional focus each day. Some people find it helpful to get up early and begin the day in quiet time with God. Others find it easier to focus late at night. Find a time that works for you, but be consistent. Communication is the key to any healthy relationship, and it is no different with God. Through prayer we talk with God, and through reading his Word we listen to his voice.

1. **Read Luke 9:23.** How often must we make the choice to follow after Jesus?

2. **Read Matthew 6:5-6.** What does this verse tell you about the importance of having quiet time with God?

3. **Read Psalm 1:2 and Psalm 119:9, 97.** How should we feel about reading God's word? Why?

4. **Read Philippians 4:8.** What is the connection between spiritual focus and the things we think about?

5. **Read Mark 1:35 and Matthew 14:23.** Was quiet time with God a priority in Jesus life? Why do you think it is important for your devotional time to be in solitude and in quietness?

Quiet Time Guide

What is a quiet time? "Quiet times" are dedicated times you set aside each day to connect with God. The goal is not just to know *about* God, but to come to *know* him as one person knows another.

STEP 1: Prepare. Before jumping into Bible reading, first prepare your heart and enter God's presence.

1. **Settle your spirit.** Be still and come to know God more deeply (Psalm 46:10).
2. **Take a deep breath.** Feel the breath of life God gave you (Genesis 2:7) and the breath of his truth he wants to breathe into you (2 Timothy 3:16-17).
3. **Meditate on the message.** Delight in God's law (Psalm 1:2).
4. **Pray for insight.** Ask God to open your eyes to see wonderful things (Psalm 119:18).
5. **Invite the Spirit.** Give the Spirit permission to bring his conviction (1 Thess. 1:5).
6. **Enter his presence.** Focus on seeking his face (Psalm 16:8; 105:4).

STEP 2: Observe. Choose a Scripture and read it 2-3 times for understanding. Observe what the passage is saying by answering the following questions with one sentence:

1. What is happening in this passage?

2. How would you describe the flow of thought?

3. What seems to be the main thought or theme?

STEP 3: Apply. More than being a hearer, we must be doers of the Word.[18]

1. **Adore**- What did you *learn about God* for which you could praise or thank him?

2. **Admit**- What did you *learn about yourself* for which you could repent?

3. **Aspire**- What did you *learn about life* that you could aspire to, ask for, and act on? What is your action plan to apply this truth to your life?

STEP 4: Pray. Take the personal conviction God has given you and pray honestly to him about it. Using the answers to the questions in Step 3, convert your application into a written prayer.

- **A**dore (praise) God for who He is (e.g. God's characteristics described in the passage you read).
- **C**onfess the sinful emotions, attitudes, and behaviors that result when we forget God.
- **T**hank God for what He has done.
- **S**upplicate (ask) God to transform you and to help you apply what He has shown you today.

STEP 5: Share. Prepare to share your insights conversationally with others. We gain tremendous benefit from hearing from the insight God has provided to each of us in our Christian walks. Give testimony from your life verse to others. Be personal, transparent, and conversational as you share. Bring to others the insight that God brought to you.

Suggested Passages to Begin
A Regular Quiet Time:

Psalm 23 – Learning to be fully satisfied in following the Lord as your Shepherd.

Matthew 11:25-30 – Finding the best life in Jesus' easy yoke.

2 Kings 6:8-17 – Having your eyes opened to the spiritual kingdom of God.

Psalm 13- Taking heart when darkness overshadows your soul.

Matthew 3:13-17 – Hearing the voice of God adopting you as his child.

Matthew 17:1-13 – Learning the power of transfiguration with Jesus in a small group.

Mark 4:35-41 – Hearing Jesus' voice of peace that calms the storms.

John 15:1-12 – Learning the life-giving power of abiding in Jesus.

Hebrews 1:1-4 – Have your heart captivated with the radiant beauty of Christ.

Revelation 4 – Be transported before the heavenly throne and driven to worship by being immersed in God's glory.

Suggested Bible Reading Selections
for New Christians:

Psalm 119

The Gospel of Mark

Galatians

Ephesians

Philippians

Colossians

1 Thessalonians

2 Thessalonians

1 Timothy

2 Timothy

Titus and Philemon

The Gospel of Luke

Acts

Romans

Genesis

James

Notes:

Part 2: Basic

Foundations of Discipleship

Welcome to BASIC: Foundations of Discipleship

"If any of you want to be my follower,
you must turn away from your selfish ways,
take up your cross daily,
and follow me."
(Luke 9:23, NLT)

The predominate message of the Bible is that we are totally dependent upon God for our salvation. We are helpless to save ourselves and must rely upon God to rescue us. This rescue came through God sending his Son as a gift (called grace). This free gift is received when we place our trust in Jesus and all he did for us (called faith). We cannot earn salvation by our works, our performance, or moral behavior. We are completely dependent upon trusting in the free gift of God's grace. But this truth of the gospel of grace might seem dangerous to some. Does salvation by grace mean obedience doesn't matter? Does grace give license to live any way we choose?

Easy Christianity?

Dietrich Bonhoeffer once warned about the danger of "cheap grace" or "easy Christianity." This is the view that you can receive the benefit of Christ's sacrifice without any commitment to Christ. This view is a horrible perversion of the gospel of grace. Grace is not only meant to provide forgiveness but also transformation of life. Once we receive the free gift of God's grace, the gift has transformative power. If you claim to be saved by grace but do not live as a disciple, you have never really accepted grace. When you really understand grace, it will not leave you as it found you. Paul makes this clear when he writes, *"For by grace you have been saved through faith. And this is not your own doing; it is the gift of God, not a result of works, so that no one may boast. For we are his workmanship, created in Christ Jesus for good works, which God prepared beforehand that we should walk in them"* (Ephesians 2:8-10). We are not saved *by* good works; but we are saved *for* good works. A.W. Tozer once expressed the concern, "that a notable heresy has come into being throughout evangelical Christian circles—the widely accepted concept that we humans can choose to accept Christ only because we need him as Savior and that we have the right to postpone our obedience to him as Lord as long as we want to!"[19] He then rightly observes, "Salvation apart from obedience is unknown in the sacred scriptures." Christianity is more than embracing a set of beliefs, it is about adopting a new lifestyle. It is a lifestyle of being an apprentice of Jesus. Following Jesus and living the "Jesus-life" is called discipleship. Discipleship is the expected product of being saved by grace. One cannot be a Christian and reject discipleship. Discipleship is not optional; it is the natural progression of the saved life.

Deciding to Follow Christ

Dallas Willard has observed, "Most problems in contemporary churches can be explained by the fact that members have not yet decided to follow Christ."[20] Willard's statement reflects the difference in simply believing in Jesus and actually following Jesus. Discipleship is more than simply believing in Jesus; it involves entering a lifelong training program learning to think as he thought and live as he lived. As Willard says, "We meet and dwell with Jesus and his Father in the disciplines for the spiritual life."[21] To become like Jesus, we must discipline ourselves in the activities into which Jesus immersed himself. With the help of the Holy Spirit, discipleship is a behavioral lifestyle that is learned and must be cultivated.

Discipleship Training

The mission of Christians is to share the message of the gospel of grace and "make disciples" (Matthew 28:19-20). But disciple-making involves more than teaching and baptism. Making disciples also includes Jesus' instruction to "teach them to observe all that I have commanded you." This has everything to do with discipleship training. Training in discipleship must include more than instruction in a set of doctrinal beliefs. To be trained in discipleship means to be mentored in how to live "the Jesus-life." Spiritual character formation into Christ-likeness comes not just by information, but by action. It is action taken under the direction of God's leading and the empowerment of his Holy Spirit.

How to Use this Study Guide

Cross Training, Part 2: BASIC is designed to be used in a group setting. A discipleship group of 3-5 people is ideal. Each lesson has two components. First is the content discussion that is designed to be a group discussion on a particular area of discipleship. At the end of the session, each participant should be encouraged to write out an action plan for the week as to how they intend to practice that particular area of discipleship. Class discussions are greatly enhanced if participants have read the lessons and done the exercises ahead of time.

At the second meeting and beyond, the group will first review the previous lesson's key concepts. Time should then be provided for each person to "check in" and discuss how their discipleship practice went during the week. Then, the group will move into the next content discussion followed by action plan development for the following week.

Discipleship takes practice and loving accountability. An important component of this approach is not just in the content but also time spent sharing your discipleship training experiences. It is vital that the person leading this study emphasize the weekly action plan and encourage each person to share each week in the life application discussion.

The format of this material requires weekly meetings of adequate length (60-90 minutes). If your meeting time is limited (perhaps a 45 minute session), it is suggested that you cover this material over two 13-week sections. You might choose 5 lessons for each section in order to reserve adequate time for discussion and reporting on weekly, discipleship challenges. The remaining three lessons (Meditate, Pray, Gospel) might be done outside of class by the students. If this is your format, I would suggest this plan:

Section 1: Study Plan
      Session 1: God
      Session 2: Close
      Session 3: Disciple
      Session 4: Inside
      Session 5: Quiet

Section 2: Study Plan
      Session 1: Train
      Session 2: Idols
      Session 3: Apply
      Session 4: Spirit
      Session 5: Share

This material can easily be used as an ongoing, cyclical gathering where new disciples enter at any point. Once a new believer enters the group, they continue the study until they complete all the lessons.

Time to Get "Cross Fit"

So put on your spiritual running shoes. It's time to stretch. This study is a personal training program for discipleship. It's time to take seriously the words of our personal trainer in the spiritual life, *"If any of you want to be my follower, you must turn away from selfish ways, take up your cross daily and follow me"* (Luke 9:23, NLT). It's time to get "cross fit." Welcome to *Cross Training*.

1

GOD

Coming to Know and Love Your Maker

Main Idea: In order to really come to know God, we must examine how God reveals himself to us. By looking at his self-descriptions, we can come to know God for who he truly is.

Bible Passages to Study This Week:

Exodus 20:4-6
You shall not make for yourself a carved image, or any likeness...You shall not bow down to them or serve them, for I the Lord your God am a jealous God.

Psalm 102:25-27
...you are the same, and your years have no end.

Exodus 3:13-15; 34:5-7
The Lord, the Lord, a God merciful and gracious, slow to anger, and abounding in steadfast love and faithfulness, keeping steadfast love for thousands, forgiving iniquity and transgression and sin, but who will by no means clear the guilty...

How Do You View God?

<u>Exodus 20:4-6</u>

What three words would you use to describe God?

1._____

2._____

3._____

When you picture God in your mind, what do you see? Do you view him as a harsh judge? A loving father? Maybe you see him as a "grandfather in the sky," or an angry miser in the clouds. When it comes to God, sometimes our imaginations run wild. Idolatry is not just the worship of false gods, it is also worshipping the true God through false images. Patrick Morley once wrote, "There is a God we want, and there is a God who is. They are not the same God. The turning point in our lives comes when we stop seeking the God we want and we start seeking the God who is."[22] The only way to really know another person is when they reveal themselves to you. God has revealed himself to us. If you really want to know God, you must let Him tell you who he is.

How might you react if your view of God was challenged?

God: The Greatest Thought

There is no greater subject that the human mind can ponder than the thought of God. No subject is more humbling, so immense, and yet so comforting. To try and live in this world without a knowledge of God is to go through life blindfolded.[23] Pondering the majesty of a God who could speak the worlds into existence is a staggering thought. Yet, as Friedrich Schiller has said, "The Universe is *one* of God's thoughts."[24] In 1990, the space probe Voyager turned and took a picture of the earth from 3.7 billion miles away. Astronomer Carl Sagan later wrote about the picture: "Look again at that dot. That's here. That's home. That's us. On it everyone you love, everyone you know, everyone you ever heard of, every human being who ever was, lived out their lives…every saint and sinner in the history of our species lived there—on a mote of dust suspended in a sunbeam…in all this vastness, there is no hint that help will come from elsewhere to save us from ourselves."[25] Contrary to the cynicism of Sagan, help has come. God has visited this "pale blue dot." And he has made himself known to the human race.

How have you been moved by the power of God in your life?

Unchanging God
Psalm 102:25-27

The Bible takes place thousands of years ago in primitive, barbaric and foreign lands.[26] It all seems so far away from our modern, scientific world. Is God the same today as he is described in the Bible? If we really stop to think about it, we would expect the Creator of the Universe to be eternal. We would expect him to be changeless and unaffected by the passage of time (which he also created). The Bible consistently affirms God's changeless nature. For instance, Psalm 102: 26-27 states that the earth and heaven "will perish, but you remain; they will all wear out like a garment. Like clothing you will change them and they will be discarded. But you remain the same, and your years will never end." Whether the Old Testament age or the New Testament, the ancient-world or the modern one, God's life, character, truth and ways do not change.

Does the idea of God's changelessness give you comfort or anxiety? Why?

The Nature of God

Exodus 3:13-15; 34:5-7

Early in the Biblical story, God reveals himself to a man named Moses in the form of a burning bush. At that time, Moses asked for God's name. God reveals his name to be "Yahweh" (corresponding to the Hebrew consonants YHWH). Most likely, these letters represent a form of the Hebrew verb meaning "to be." So most translations say God responded, "I am who I am" (Exodus 3:14). This name suggests God's self-existence and his eternal changelessness. Throughout the Bible, God's name is often translated "LORD."

Later on the same mountain, God again emphasizes his changelessness by stressing that he is the "LORD" and then he describes his character. God reveals his nature in Exodus 34:5-7 in several ways:

He is a person with a name. He is the "LORD" (Yahweh). Revealing his name shows us that he wants to relate.

He is merciful and gracious. He is compassionate to hurting and suffering people.

He is slow to anger. He does not have a short fuse. He is long-suffering and patient with us.

He is consistently loving. His love for us abounds and his compassion toward us is relentless.

He is dependable and truthful. He can be trusted. You never have to question his motives or his integrity.

He is quick to forgive. He does not hold grudges. He wants to forgive and desires to heal broken relationships.

He is just. He cannot overlook injustice, wrongdoing, and unrepentant sin. God is always fair and desires to right the wrongs in our world.

Which of these traits most challenge your concept of God? (Pick one, meditate upon it for the week, write your thoughts below and be prepared to share them in the next session).

Invited into God's Circle

When God first created human beings, he revealed himself to be a complex being. He said, "Let us make man in our image" (Genesis 1:26). Although the Bible consistently affirms that there is but one God, he often reveals himself using plural pronouns. The complex nature of God is only partially revealed in the Old Testament, but is more fully made known in the New Testament (Matthew 3:16-17; 28:19; 2 Corinthians 13:14; Ephesians 4:4-6; 1 Peter 1:2). The one God exists in three persons—Father, Son, Holy Spirit. From all eternity, God has existed in a community of mutual love. God, by his very nature, is relational. He created us to expand the circle of his love. And he invites us all to enter into this circle.

 How does it make you feel to know God wants to embrace you into his family?

Key Concepts in this Lesson:

◆ God has revealed himself to humanity.

◆ Our view of God must be shaped by how he has revealed himself.

◆ Being eternal in nature, God's life, character, truth and ways are unchanging.

◆ The true God wants to relate to us, is merciful and gracious, is slow to anger, is loving and dependable, is quick to forgive and is just.

Prepare for Next Week's Discussion:
How might you live this out?

In your class or small group, brainstorm some ways to live out this aspect of discipleship. Here are a few ideas to get started:

◆ **Using the descriptions of God explored in this lesson, meditate deeply on each characteristic.** Find a quiet place and think deeply on each trait of God, and allow your heart to come to know God for who he really is. Take notes of your thoughts.

◆ **Discipline yourself to sit in 5 minutes of silence and pay careful attention to the created world.** What does the world around you reveal about the nature of the true God?

◆ **Consider what "projected images" you might be imposing upon God.** How might your relationship with your father, mother, spouse, or children impact your view of God? How might you be imposing a false image upon God?

Your action plan for this week:

_____

_____

_____

_____

_____

_____

_____

_____

_____

_____

_____

Want to dig deeper on this topic?
A recommended resource:
J.I. Packer. *Knowing God.* (Downer's Grove: IVP, 1973).

Group Check In:

What was your action plan for knowing God this week?

How did things go?

What did you learn about God?

What did you learn about yourself?

Notes:

2

CLOSE

Drawing Near in a Personal Relationship

Main Idea: Jesus came to provide a means for us to know God in a close and personal way. More than simply knowing things *about* God, the purpose of our existence is to come to *know* God in intimate friendship.

Bible Passages to Study This Week:

Acts 17:22-31
...that they should seek God, and perhaps feel their way toward him and find him. Yet he is actually not far from each one of us.

John 15:12-15
No longer do I call you servants...but I have called you friends.

John 17:1-3
And this is eternal life, that they may know you the only true God, and Jesus Christ, whom you have sent.

1 Corinthians 6:15-20
But he who is joined to the Lord becomes one spirit with him.

Close Friendships

How would you describe your closest friendship?
What makes you so close to that friend?

We all long for deep connection with others. But for this to happen, we must take the risk of friendship. Close friendships require trust and vulnerability. But if we want to know the beauty of friendship, we must open ourselves up to being close to others.

Have you ever considered the idea that you can have a close friendship with God? As we discovered in the previous lesson, God is always faithful and trustworthy. He encourages us to "draw near" to him with full assurance (Hebrews 10:22). Beyond just believing in God, he invites us into an intimate relationship with him.

What might it take for you to experience God as a friend?

Far or Near?

Acts 17:22-31

When Paul came to Athens, he found people who were very religious. And he found people who spent considerable time thinking about the meaning of life and the power behind it all. While they were very religious, a personal relationship with the true God was "unknown" to them. Paul reveals that we can seek God, find him, and actually come to know that he is not far but is near to us. We live, move and exist in God's presence, and we can be close to him.

How "impersonal" or "personal" is God to you? Explain.

Knowing About God
or Knowing God?
John 15:12-15

When you begin to learn about God, you need to ask yourself a very important question: What is my ultimate aim and objective in occupying my mind with these things? What do you intend to do with your knowledge of God, once you obtain it?[27] Theological knowledge on its own can be spiritually damaging. Knowledge alone can easily make a person arrogant and prideful (1 Corinthians 8:1-2). In fact, religion can actually be the means by which a person actually avoids a real relationship with God. The real aim of studying about God is not to simply know *about* him, but to actually come to *know* God himself better. The entire purpose of Jesus' ministry was to provide a way that we could come to know real friendship with God. Imagine living your life with the confidence that God calls you "friend."

In your opinion, what is the difference between knowing "about" God and actually "knowing" God personally?

The Very Purpose of Life
John 17:1-3

We all seem to have the same itch. Within us we long for something more. No matter how we try to find fulfillment in life, it feels like there is something missing. We were originally created to enjoy deep spiritual friendship with God. But when Adam and Eve sinned, the friendship was severed and they hid from God (Genesis 3:8). But God sent Jesus as the means of restoring that friendship. In fact, Jesus says that is the very definition of "eternal life"—to know deep connection and friendship with God.

In what ways have you tried to find purpose and meaning in your life?

How to Know God

Really knowing another person is always dependent upon self-disclosure. God makes himself known to us through the natural creation, life's circumstances, and especially through Scripture. He allows us to know him by initiating the conversation. To deeply come to know God, we must immerse ourselves into his message to humanity. The Bible is God's autobiography, his self-disclosure to us. The primary goal of all true Bible study should be to have deeper intimacy with God. We must search out the Scriptures to learn the mind and heart of God in order to come to know him for who he truly is (cf. John 5:39-42). More than simply knowing the Word of the Lord, we must come to know the Lord of the Word.[28]

Draw Near to God
<u>1 Corinthians 6:15-20</u>

Though not a perfect comparison, perhaps one of the best ways to think about your relationship with God is in terms of dating and marriage. When you first fall in love with someone, your thoughts are focused on that person. You savor every conversation and look forward to every meeting. When you are in love, your thoughts are ever upon the object of your love. The beautiful thing about divine romance, is that your love for God will never go unreturned. The Bible promises, "Draw near to God, and he will draw near to you" (James 4:8). God is relentless in his pursuit of us. As R. Kent Hughes says, "The soul-tingling truth is here, if you go after God, he will go after you!...Inch toward God, and he will step toward you. Step toward God, and he will sprint toward you. Sprint toward God, and he will fly to you!"[29]

Perhaps the text that most emphasizes a personal relationship with Jesus is 1 Corinthians 6:17. Here, we are warned not to engage in sexual immorality because sexual intercourse involves not only a physical, but a spiritual union of people (vs. 17). Then we are reminded, "But he who is joined to the Lord becomes one spirit with him." This is true because the Spirit of God resides in the physical body of the baptized believer (vs. 19; cf. 1 Cor. 12:13). Using the spiritual union of husbands and wives in marriage, Paul teaches that this same intimate union exists between Christ and his followers (Ephesians 5:31-32). In his commentary on Galatians, Martin Luther observed, "Faith connects you so intimately with Christ, that He and you become as it were one person."[30] It is all about being close to God. It is about a personal relationship with him.

What are some ways that relationship with God might be similar to romantic relationships?

Key Concepts in this lesson:

♦ God is seeking a close, intimate friendship with you.

♦ Rather than being distant and removed, God wants to be near to you.

♦ The goal of Christian faith is not just knowledge about God, but personal knowledge of him.

♦ God has made himself known to us in the Bible and is relentless in his pursuit to have a friendship with us.

Prepare for Next Week's Discussion:
How might you live this out?

In your class or small group, brainstorm some ways to live out this aspect of discipleship. Here are a few ideas to get started:

♦ **Write out a personal prayer to God.** In the prayer, ask God to help you discover a deeper, more personal relationship with him.

♦ **Deliberately try to *practice the presence of God* this week.** Challenge yourself in the discipline of being aware of God's presence in your daily routine. See how many times per hour you are aware of God.

♦ **Pray Psalm 23.**[31] This is a psalm written for daily living. Memorize the psalm and recite it throughout the day. Meditate on each word. Allow the images in this psalm to wash over you. Allow the true nature of who God is to imbed into your soul.

Your action plan for this week:

_____

_____

_____

_____

_____

_____

_____

_____

_____

_____

_____

_____

_____

Want to dig deeper on this topic?

A recommended resource:

Kenneth Boa. *Life in the Presence of God.* (Downer's Grove: IVP, 2017).

Group Check In:

What was your action plan for drawing close to God this week?

How did things go?

What did you learn about God?

What did you learn about yourself?

3

DISCIPLE

The Life Commitment of Following Jesus

Main Idea: Jesus calls us to follow him and be his disciples. Discipleship is when we joyfully model our lives after Jesus and delight in attempting to live like him.

Bible Passages to Study This Week:

Luke 9:23-25

And he said to all, "If anyone would come after me, let him deny himself and take up his cross daily and follow me."

Luke 6:46-49

Why do you call me "Lord, Lord" and do not do what I say?

Who Do You Follow?

<u>Luke 9:23-25</u>

Who is an author, celebrity, politician, radio personality, podcast host, that you tend to follow on a regular basis? Why do you follow them?

For some of us, it is a favorite radio or television host. For others, it is a favorite sports show, a podcast, or a particular author. Maybe you follow a Twitter feed or have liked a celebrity's Facebook page. Perhaps you follow the career of a professional football player or watch the work of a politician with great interest. You may have a parent, a teacher, or a mentor you look up to. Regardless of the specifics, we all follow someone. Jesus invites us all to come and really follow him.

What does it mean to you to follow Jesus?

What is a Disciple?

Millions of people today on this earth call themselves followers of Jesus. Yet for many, their lives look nothing like Jesus. C.S. Lewis once warned that the word "Christian" might one day become a useless description.[32] He warned that the term might become "spoiled" by using it to describe a "good" person (a gentleman) or a religious person without any connection to actually being a disciple of Jesus. The call of being a disciple is not about trying to be a good, moral person. Doing religious things does not make you a disciple. In fact, discipleship is not less than believing in Jesus, but it is more. When Jesus says, "Follow me," he does not mean "Admire me." Jesus is calling us to fully embrace his life's teachings, totally commit to him, and model our lives after his own. The word "Christian" is never used by Jesus and is only found 3 times in the entire Bible. Meanwhile, the word "disciple" occurs nearly 270 times in the New Testament. Jesus is serious about us really following him. We are to be his apprentices. Discipleship is not optional and is not reserved for "super Christians." Jesus says to us all, "Follow me."

In what sense might a person consider themselves a Christian without being a disciple of Jesus?

How might the term "Christian" have been spoiled in common usage today?

Discipleship is About Self-Denial

According to Jesus, discipleship involves both self-denial and taking up your cross daily. To "deny" yourself means that you say "no" to yourself and "yes" to God. Self-denial is about surrendering your will to God. Why would anyone voluntarily choose to forfeit their will to God? Jesus reveals that when you "lose" your life for his sake, you will truly find life (Luke 9:24). We were originally created by God for maximum joy and life.[33] But Adam and Eve sinned, humankind turned inward and selfishness was ignited in our hearts. With sin, self-regard rose to supreme importance in the human heart. Most of the evil in this fallen world originates from selfishness. Jesus wants to restore the original joy of Paradise for us; but such requires self-denial. Self-denial paves the way for restoring the beauty of life we were designed to enjoy. When we deny ourselves, we are sacrificing our personal good for the good of others (the greater good). Self-denial is not about denying yourself pleasure. Rather it is about choosing the greater pleasure. It is about the greater good. Choosing the joy for which you were created. It is choosing a life in harmony with your divine design. We were made in God's image and created for relationships. For relationships to flourish, we must shift the focus away from ourselves and place it upon others. You were made for intimate relationship with God, other human beings, and creation itself. You will only come to experience the abundant life for which you were made when you choose to be outward focused. So the real measure of your discipleship is the extent to which you have denied yourself.[34] Self-denial is not always relinquishing your will over to the will of others, but it is always about surrendering your will to God's will.

From a practical standpoint, what might a life of self-denial look like?

What examples from your life might illustrate self-denial?

Other examples:

- Suppose someone hurts you. Your natural reaction is to get angry and lash out. Discipleship denies this impulse and forgives your enemy.

- Dying to self means you no longer try to get your own way or try to get people to look up to you. You give up trying to impress others.

- You stop offering unasked-for advice, as if in your self-importance you always know better than others.

- Put simply, when you die to self you are no longer obsessed with self.[35]

Following the Leader

Luke 6:46-49

Being a disciple means you follow Jesus. Jesus lived a life of self-denial, always putting the needs of others before himself. Jesus says, "Follow me." Francis Chan gives a great illustration of what that really looks like.[36] As kids, most of us played "Follow the Leader." You were only following the leader if you did what the leader was doing. It would be ridiculous to say, "I'm raising my hand in my heart." Imagine that a child is told by a parent, "Go clean your room." It is not enough for the child to come back an hour later and say, "I memorized what you said," or "I met with some friends to discuss what it would look like if we cleaned our rooms," or "I can say 'clean your room' in Greek." The child has only followed when they actually cleaned the room. Being a disciple is more than just believing what Jesus taught. Discipleship is all about following the leader—Jesus.

Imitating Your Parent

It is often humorous to watch young children trying to imitate their parents. Each morning, my son always wanted to know what I was going to wear. Then he would go to his closet and pick out clothes that looked most like mine. He then would come back beaming, so proud that he looked like his dad. Really, the same is true of following Jesus. Discipleship is when we joyfully model our lives after Jesus (our parent), and delight in attempting to live like him.

When was the last time you felt Jesus nudging you to do something, and you turned to your own way?

Key Concepts in this lesson:

♦ Following Jesus is more than calling yourself a Christian—it means being a disciple of his life.

♦ A disciple uses Jesus' life as a model or template for his/her own attitudes and actions.

♦ The measure of your discipleship is the extent to which you have denied yourself.

♦ More than making a decision to believe in Jesus, we must make a commitment to follow him.

Prepare for Next Week's Discussion:
How might you live this out?

In your class or small group, brainstorm some ways to live out this aspect of discipleship. Here are a few ideas to get started:

♦ **Really listen when other people are talking.** Instead of letting your mind wander, allow yourself to be completely absorbed in someone else's world.

♦ **Think about how other people feel.** Imagine yourself in other people's situations. Try and understand how someone else feels, and be moved to act selflessly toward that person.

♦ **Don't value your time more than other people's.** Practice patience toward others.

Your action plan for this week:

_____

_____

_____

_____

_____

_____

_____

_____

_____

_____

_____

_____

_____

_____

Want to dig deeper on this topic?

A recommended resource:
Kyle Idleman. *Not a Fan: Becoming a Completely Committed Follower of Jesus.* (Grand Rapids: Zondervan, 2011).

Group Check In:

What was your action plan for discipleship this week?

How did things go?

What did you learn about God?

What did you learn about yourself?

4

INSIDE

<u>Nourishing and Maintaining Your Inner Self</u>

Main Idea: Every person lives in two worlds: the public (outer) world and the private (inner) world. You must not neglect your inner self, but instead build a strong spiritual foundation for the real you.

Bible Passages to Study This Week:

Luke 6:43-45
A good person brings out good things from the treasure of his heart.

Matthew 7:24-27
Everyone who hears these words of mine and does them will be like a wise man who built his house on a rock.

Proverbs 4:23
Above all else, guard your heart, for it is the wellspring of life.

The Inner You

Luke 6:43-45

Who in your life, more than anyone else, knows the "real you?"

Fatigue. Failure. Exhaustion. Sometimes the weight of life's burdens make us feel like something deep within is about to give way.[37] Have you ever felt that you were on the brink of a total collapse? Have you ever felt you were only moments away from being exposed for who you "really are"? Most of life is spent on the visible level, where urgent things call for our undivided attention. Meanwhile, there is an invisible level to life—our private world—that can quietly be neglected. In life, it is not enough to simply keep our outer worlds organized, neat and tidy. We must also clean the inside of the cup. We must maintain, nourish, and develop our inner selves. Why? Because when you are under pressure, the person you "really" are on the inside will be revealed to the outside world.

What tends to get more attention in your life, the urgent or the important? Is there a difference? If so, how would you explain the difference?

Two Worlds

We must all realize that we live in two very different worlds. The "outer world" is our public persona that is visible to everyone. This world is easy to deal with and is more measurable and visible. Things like work, hobbies, family, possessions, church involvement, and the house we live in are all in the outer world. This is the part of life that is most often evaluated for success.

But the "inner world" is the place where choices are made, where we hold our values and convictions, and where solitude and reflection take place. All true worship and true confession begins in the inner world. It is the place of rest, character, and prayer.

Our "outer worlds" scream for attention and demand immediate action. Meanwhile, our "inner worlds" can be neglected for long periods of time with seemingly no ill effect. But if the inner world is neglected long enough, you will not be strong enough to carry the stressful demands the outer world places upon you.

What decisions might you make to strengthen your "inner world?"

A Strong Foundation

Matthew 7:24-27

Why do you think God is so concerned about our hearts, as opposed to the outer appearance?

Most all of life focuses on the "outer world." But while people focus on the outer appearance, God is very concerned with our inner wellbeing (1 Samuel 16:7). People of character and integrity are careful to maintain their "inner worlds." If you don't want to buckle under the pressure of life, make it a priority to build and maintain the foundation of your inner world. Jesus compares a neglect of the inner self to building your house on the sand. If your inner world has been neglected when the difficult days come and the storms blow, you are headed for a nervous breakdown, a spiritual implosion. But if you have built your life on good spiritual principles taught by Jesus, you can endure the days of the storm.

In what ways have you been tempted to build your life on sand? On rock?

The Real You

<u>Proverbs 4:23</u>

When we talk about a person's "heart," what are we normally thinking about?

When we think of the "heart," we usually think almost exclusively about the emotions. But in the Bible, the heart is the inner self that thinks, feels, and decides.[38] Biblically, the heart is what is central to the person. It is the place of emotions, thinking, character, and personality. The heart is the "inner world"—the real you. God directs us to guard our hearts carefully because all of life springs forth from the heart.

D.L. Moody once said, "Character is what you are in the dark."[39] That is, the real you is the person that you are when no one else is looking. The substance of "the real you" is determined by your thoughts. Timothy Keller wrote, "To discover the real you, look at what you spend time thinking about when no one is looking, when nothing is forcing you to think about anything in particular."[40] Where does your mind naturally and instinctively go when you have nothing to focus upon? The thing that your mind settles upon is your real religion, your real god, the thing upon which you are truly placing your faith. What are you building your thoughts and your life upon? Is the real you built on a false god (founded on sand) or the true God who is a rock?

Honestly examine your own heart. Where does your mind naturally go when you have nothing to focus upon?

What Rises to the Top?

"The real you" is revealed when you are under pressure. How do you respond when you are suddenly in a fender bender? The waitress pours a drink in your lap, how do you react? When someone bumps into us in life, the person we are on the inside spills out. Whatever spills out in that moment demonstrates what really fills your life. Are you filled with God's spirit or your own sinful nature?

Since you became a Christian, how have your natural reactions changed when you are under pressure? Have they?

Key Concepts in this lesson:

♦ We all live in two worlds: the outer world that is visible to others and the inner world that is spiritual in nature.

♦ While our outer selves scream for attention, our inner selves are easily neglected.

♦ To withstand the strain and storms of life, we must build our inner selves upon the spiritual teachings of Jesus.

♦ We must carefully guard our hearts, the seat of our emotions, decisions, thinking, and character.

Prepare for Next Week's Discussion:
How might you live this out?

In your class or small group, brainstorm some ways to live out this aspect of discipleship. Here are a few ideas to get started:

♦ **Make a list of the most important things in your life.**[41] Of all of your responsibilities, what things can only you do? What things do you repeatedly do that could be delegated to others? List the top 5 things that you must not neglect in your life.

♦ **Discipline yourself to have a regular quiet time for spiritual reflection each day this week.** Pick a place and time and do not miss this important meeting for an entire week.

♦ **Spiritually evaluate your inner world.** Brainstorm the top 3 areas in your life where you most need to be spiritually strengthened. Develop an action plans for one of them. How can this area be strengthened in your life?

Your action plan for this week:

_____

_____

_____

_____

_____

_____

_____

_____

_____

_____

_____

Want to dig deeper on this topic?

A recommended resource:

John Ortberg. *Soul Keeping: Caring for the Most Important Part of You.* (Grand Rapids: Zondervan, 2014).

Group Check In:

What was your action plan for your "inner self" this week?

How did things go?

What did you learn about God?

What did you learn about yourself?

5

MEDITATE

Main Idea: Spiritual health and wellbeing require that we slow down and intentionally create time and space for spiritual focus in our lives.

Bible Passages to Study This Week:

Exodus 20:8-10
Six days you shall labor and do all your work, but the seventh day is a sabbath of the Lord your God; in it you shall not do any work....

Psalm 46:10
Be still and know that I am God.

Psalm 127:2
It is in vain that you rise up early and go late to rest, eating the bread of anxious toil.

Matthew 6:16-18
And when you fast...

Psalm 1
...and on his law he meditates day and night.

Overloaded

Exodus 20:8-10

When in your life have you felt completely burned out and exhausted?

Your soul is like a battery.[42] Every time you give life away to others, your battery is discharged. In order to keep running, your battery needs to be recharged regularly. But recharging your soul is not something that happens quickly—it's a slow, gradual recharge that takes dedicated time.

When God gave a top ten list of spiritual instructions, a deliberate day of rest was among them. As important as "do not murder" or "have no other gods before me" is "keep the Sabbath day holy." Debating religious rituals and days often misses the spiritual truth God is trying to communicate to us. We are busy creatures, and God knew he would have to make us slow down, stop, and reflect on spiritual reality. We must discipline ourselves to have times of rest for spiritual (holy) purposes. Recharging the soul by connecting with God is needed on a consistent and regular basis. Meditation helps orient our lives and cultivate a holistic vision that the spiritual permeates every aspect of our lives.

What might be the difference in taking a "vacation" of rest and taking a "holy" rest?

Slow Down & Be Still

Psalm 46:10

On a scale of 1-10 (with 1 being a turtle and 10 being a cheetah), what would you say is the current pace of your life?

The angelic, soprano voices of the temple singers (likely indicated by the prefixed inscription) praised God for the deliverance he provided from their enemies. They sang the words of Psalm 46 to remember how God had sent his angel to fight the battle that delivered Israel from the brutal Assyrian army. This Psalm recounts how the people were terrified when they were surrounded by turmoil and uncertainty. God calms their fears and says, *"Be still and know that I am God."* He commands his people to relax, be calm and trust that he will be their fortress in time of trouble. We can rise above the fray by resting in God's presence. We must stop our striving and hand-wringing, and come to know God's power and presence. We will never come to know God until we learn to be still. Connecting with God is nearly impossible when his voice is crowded out by all the noise in our lives. We must shut out all the background noise of life, be still, and come to know God.

How do you think learning to be still is related to coming to know God?

Room in the Margin?

Psalm 127:2

What determines the pace at which you live your life?

One of the greatest things that hinders dynamic spiritual life today is exhaustion.[43] Holiness in life is difficult, if not impossible, if we don't feel a sense of wholeness. Today many Christians feel constantly in a hurry with overloaded schedules. Many of us suffer from "hurry sickness."[44] We continually run out the clock and live life to the edge. Our culture today is hyperactive. We are always multi-tasking, and we train ourselves to have attention deficit disorder. Few of us leave any room in the margin of our lives. As a result, we feel tired, lonely, joyless, and leave ourselves vulnerable to temptation.[45] We must learn to slow down, eliminate unnecessary things in our lives, stop overextending our abilities, and create space for ourselves, our families, our health, and God. Sometimes getting up early, going to bed late, and working our fingers to the bone doesn't result in getting ahead but rather puts us further behind (Psalm 127:2). Creating space in the margin is crucial for spiritual wellness.

What changes might make your life simpler but more rich and fulfilling?

Fasting: Learning to Say No

Matthew 6:16-18

How do you think fasting might draw you closer to God?

Have you ever been without electricity for several days? Without electricity, lights, television, and internet, the swift pace of life suddenly slows to a crawl. *Fasting* from the speediness of modern culture can become a *feast* of realizing what is most important. Fasting is a spiritual practice that permeates the Bible. Jesus assumed his followers would fast (Matthew 6:16-18). Fasting is basically the practice of saying "no" to things in your life in order to gain focus and clarity. It is not limited to food but also includes things like denying yourself certain pleasures for a limited time (cf. 1 Corinthians 7:5).

Fasting generally has to do with short bursts of intentional focus. We need this practice periodically. However, think of this principle on a larger plane. Sometimes we also need to reprioritize our lives. For real focus, sometimes we may need to permanently "fast" from things that are distracting us. The only way to prevent overload, slow the pace of life, and create margin is to prioritize your schedule and learn to say "no" to some things. It is not always about choosing good things over bad. In order to make spiritual focus a priority, sometimes we must eliminate unnecessary things and choose the best things even over other good things. Spiritual wellbeing requires making room for and giving priority to your spiritual life.

How might you better embrace a holistic perspective that the spiritual permeates every aspect of your life?

The Power of Meditation

<u>Psalm 1</u>

What things in your life are most likely to consume your mind?

Everyone meditates on something. If you worry, you know how to meditate.[46] Constant meditation on your problems will ruin you. Some religions teach meditation, breathing techniques, and emptying the mind to escape the problems and release the stress of life. In the Bible, meditation is not about emptying the mind, but filling the mind with the right things (cf. Colossians 3:16).

When you meditate on spiritual things, it provides stability to the soul. Like a tree planted by a stream, you will be stable in dry times because your life is rooted in a divine source. Like a tree that bears fruit, a person who meditates on spiritual things has deep convictions and draws from wisdom rather than living by whim and impulse. By focusing your mind on spiritual things, there is a sustained, continual growth. As you meditate on God's instructions day and night, the truths of life will sink into your soul and gradually grow you into a person of wisdom and character.

Is meditation a regular part of your life? If so, what do you tend to meditate upon?

Key Concepts in this lesson:

- Spiritual health requires disciplining ourselves to have times of rest for spiritual (holy) purposes.
- Coming to really know God relationally requires slowing down, being still, and quieting your spirit.
- We must learn to say "no" to some things in life in order to create margin and space for spiritual focus.
- Spiritual strength and character is developed by consistently filling the mind (meditating) on God's instructions.

Prepare for Next Week's Discussion:
How might you live this out?

In your class or small group, brainstorm some ways to live out this aspect of discipleship. Here are a few ideas to get started:

- **Choose a short passage of Scripture to memorize this week.** Throughout the week, recall the passage and then meditate upon it. *Think out* the truth the verses contain and then *think it into* your life. Consider the various implications of the truth. Allow the truths of the verses to wash over you and sink into your heart.

- **Pick something in your life to eliminate this week. Replace that space with something spiritual.** Rather than watching an hour of television, you might spend an hour in Bible study or prayer journaling. Instead of eating alone during your lunch break, go to lunch with a coworker with the intention of developing a better relationship.

Your action plan for this week:

_____

_____

_____

_____

_____

_____

_____

_____

_____

_____

_____

Want to dig deeper on this topic?

A recommended resource:

John Ortberg. *Soul Keeping: Caring for the Most Important Part of You.* (Grand Rapids: Zondervan, 2014).

Group Check In:

What was your action plan for your meditation this week?

How did things go?

What did you learn about God?

What did you learn about yourself?

Notes:

6

QUIET

Deeply Connecting with God

Main Idea: Connection with God occurs when we make specific and deliberate time to meet with him in prayer. When we reserve focused, uninterrupted time with God, we experience the reward of intimate relationship with him.

Bible Passages to Study This Week:

Luke 11:1
Lord teach us to pray.

Matthew 6:5-15
But when you pray, go into your room and close the door and pray to your Father in secret. And your Father who sees in secret will reward you.

Learning to Pray Well

Luke 11:1

How did you first learn how to pray?

"Now I lay me down to sleep, I pray the Lord my soul to keep…" "God is great, God is good, let us thank him for our food…." Maybe you learned to first pray using one of these formula prayers or one similar. Most people learn to pray by listening to others. Hearing others pray, we may pick up good or bad praying habits. From our earliest days, the type of prayers many are taught are very self-focused. We pray, "help *me*," "bless *me*," "keep *me*." Maybe you have quit praying because you did not get the answers you wanted. But what if this wasn't the point of prayer at all? What if prayer isn't primarily about your needs and desires? What if the way we have learned to pray is wrong?[47]

What would you say is the purpose of prayer?

Is there more to prayer?

The way Jesus prayed was different, and his disciples noticed. Once after he finished praying, his followers said, "Lord, teach us to pray" (Luke 11:1). Jesus had a special connection with God, and it showed. Jesus' followers were religious men who had prayed their entire lives. But maybe they had been praying wrong. You can pray your entire life and not really know anything about it. Jesus' disciples knew that there was more to prayer than they had ever known. They wanted to know more. Do you? Before you can learn to pray, you might first have to unlearn prayer.

Who do you know in your life that seems to have a deep connection with God? What is it about their life, in your opinion, that makes that deep connection possible?

The "Place" You Pray Matters
Matthew 6:5-15

We might assume that effective praying involves the right words and the right length. Yet, Jesus shows us that the words we choose or the length of our prayers do not gain us favor with God (Matthew 6:7). Surprisingly, Jesus focuses on the place where we pray. While it is true that we can pray anywhere and anytime (1 Thessalonians 5:17), Jesus wants something deeper for our prayers. He tells his followers not to love praying on the street corners or in front of large crowds. Rather, we should "go into your room, close the door, and pray in secret" (Matt. 6:6). He teaches us to go somewhere by ourselves, to a specific spot, close out all the distractions and connect with God. If we want to come to really know God, we must first "be still" and get quiet (Psalm 46:10). Jesus modeled this for us in his prayer life when he slipped away from the crowds into solitude and prayed (Matthew 14:23; Mark 1:35). To make deep connection with God, we must get alone just with him.

Why do you think Jesus would teach us to "go into your room and close the door" to pray? How could this "alone time with God" be accomplished in your life?

Prayer is Relationship with God

In marriage, it is possible to have everyday conversation with your spouse but feel completely disconnected relationally. There is a tremendous difference in doing life together (bills, dinner, homework, ball practice) and really connecting. We make demands, have requests, and pass on daily information through the chaos of life. But for intimacy and connection of relationship to occur, husbands and wives need time alone together. Marriage is somewhat of a mirror of the kind of relationship God wants with us. You can talk to God all your life in prayer and not feel connected to him. For connection to occur, "Go into your room, and close the door."

What might be the difference between talking with someone and connecting with someone?

The Reward of Prayer

Jesus says that when you pray in your room with the door shut, God will "see" you and "reward" you. The reward of prayer is not in getting requests answered. In fact, Jesus says God already knows what you need before you ask (Matthew 5:8). He teaches us not to spend too much time asking for stuff that God already knows that we need. We are not informing God of anything when we pray. Why pray then? What if prayer is not as much about making requests as it about connection and relationship with God? One author puts it this way, "Prayer is a way of walking in love with God."[48] The reward of prayer is that God "sees" you; and when you get alone with him, you might just catch a glimpse of him too. We must "seek God's face" (Psalm 27:8; 105:4). Prayer is about coming into God's presence (Psalm 16:8). Before we ever ask for anything from God's hand, we must first realize the purpose of prayer is to seek God's face.[49] Connection with God is the greatest reward of prayer. The reward is the peace and comfort of God's presence.

Share a time when you have earnestly sought a deep connection with God. Did you perceive he was present? What led you to this belief?

Key Concepts in this Lesson:

- It is possible to pray your entire life and not really know how to pray.
- Deep relationship with God in prayer is not necessarily about the right words, but the right "location" could make a big difference.
- The real reward of prayer is not receiving requests from God but connecting in intimate relationship with him.

<u>Prepare for Next Week's Discussion:</u>
How might you live this out?

In your class or small group, brainstorm some ways to live out this aspect of discipleship. Here are a few ideas to get started:

- **Block out a specific time each day to do nothing but meet with God.** Rather than "praying on the go," make some deliberate and specific time to seek God's face.

- **Work on moving your prayers from being "request-based" to being "worship-based."** Instead of focusing on yourself, your requests, and your desires, spend time relishing in God's presence and praising him for his beauty and glory. Choose Psalm 5, 95 or 103 and read it slowly. Put this psalm into your own words and use it as a prayer to God.

- **Move away from a "prayer list" toward a spiritual prayer journal of encounters with God.** Rather than trying to use prayer to get God to do our will in heaven, use prayer as a means to ask God to do his will on earth.

Your action plan for this week:

_____

_____

_____

_____

_____

_____

_____

_____

_____

_____

_____

Want to dig deeper on this topic?

A recommended resource:

Daniel Henderson. *Transforming Prayer.* (Minneapolis: Bethany, 2011).

Group Check In:

What was your action plan for quietness this week?

How did things go?

What did you learn about God?

What did you learn about yourself?

7

PRAY

The Pathway to Deeper Relationship with God

Main Idea: Prayer is a divinely given tool for us to pursue deep relationship and connection with God. Rather than being primarily a means of getting things from God, prayer is the way we align our will to his divine will.

Bible Passages to Study This Week:

Matthew 6:9-13
Pray then like this…

Matthew 26:36-46
…he fell on his face and prayed, saying, "My Father, if it be possible, let this cup pass from me; nevertheless, not as I will, but as you will."

Hebrews 5:7-8
In the days of his flesh, Jesus offered up prayers and supplications, with loud cries and tears, to him who was able to save him from death, and he was heard because of his reverence. Although he was a son, he learned obedience through what he suffered.

Learning How to Pray
Matthew 6:9-13

When you pray, on what do you usually spend most of your time?

Jesus teaches his followers how to pray by giving an example. Unfortunately, many Christians have used this prayer as a formula to be memorized. Yet, on another occasion Jesus quotes this prayer differently, omitting several phrases (see Luke 11:2-4). Rather than being a formula to be memorized, Jesus gives us a template to follow in the construction of our own personal prayers. Deep connection with God in prayer is not about the right choice of words or the length of the prayer. It is more about the priority, the pattern and the order. Jesus outlines three stages of prayer and emphasizes an order of priority.[50]

How have you seen the Lord's prayer most often used by Christians?

First, declare God's glory

"Our Father who is in heaven, hallowed be your name"

For most of us, our tendency is to begin with our needs in prayer. Rather than starting with you, Jesus teaches that we should start with God. He invites us to call God "Our Father." Prayer must begin by recognizing to whom we are talking. God welcomes us into a warm, family relationship—he is our "Father." But he is also "in heaven," so we must also declare his greatness. God's name is "hallowed"—he is great and to be honored. The more time that you spend recognizing to whom you are talking, the less you will be concerned about your wants, needs, and desires. Recognizing the greatness of our heavenly Father puts our problems into proper perspective. When we understand God better, we understand ourselves better. Prayer must begin with declaring God's glory. We must not rush by this. Don't proceed to the next stages of prayer until you have allowed God's greatness to sink into your heart.

How might spending significant time declaring God's glory at the beginning change the rest of your prayer?

Second, surrender your will

"Your kingdom come, your will be done"

When we pray, we often want to rush to "my will, my needs, my wishes." But before making requests, surrender "your kingdom purpose" over to God's. Get to a place in your spirit where you are content with God's will no matter the answer to your specific requests. Work hard to say to God, "I am surrendering all of me to all of you… your agenda comes before my agenda…I am fully surrendered to your will for my life." The real point of prayer is not to get stuff from God but to get our hearts into alignment with his will for our lives. Before proceeding to your requests, stay in the surrender stage of prayer until you are able to really do it. Sometimes this takes a while. The night of his betrayal, Jesus himself wrestled all night to surrender to God's will (Matthew 26:36-46). The condition of our heart can, at times, affect the length of our prayers. Pray that God's heavenly purpose would be done in your life on earth.

Why do you think we, at times, have difficulty surrendering our wills over to God?

Third, acknowledge your dependency

"Give us our daily bread...forgive our debts...lead us not into temptation but deliver us from evil"

Each remaining aspect of this prayer reflects an awareness of dependency upon God. We must acknowledge our dependency upon God's daily provision for our physical and spiritual needs. Jesus' original audience would have remembered how their ancestors depended upon daily bread from heaven (manna) in the wilderness. God provided all the bread needed for that specific day, and they were dependent upon it. Later, God promised to bless them with great abundance (Deuteronomy 8:3-14). Whether we have a little or a lot, we must not forget that it all comes from God. By asking God for these things, we declare our dependence upon him for daily needs, pardon from sin, and spiritual protection.

How might acknowledging your dependence upon God impact your relationship with him?

An Abrupt Ending

Some translations of the Bible include a different ending to the prayer: "for thine is the kingdom, power, glory...." Since the translation of the King James Version in 1611, older manuscripts have been discovered which demonstrate that this ending was added later by scribes.

Originally, Jesus' model prayer ended abruptly: "and lead us not into temptation, Amen." The prayer is rather short, but again it is not necessarily about the words. Rather, we should consider the order, the priority, the pattern. Prayer is about: declaring God's glory, surrendering your will, and acknowledging your dependency. Jesus says, "Pray like this." Prayer that deeply connects must start with God and end with you. But what comes in between is the key—surrendering your will. Have you ever really said to God, "Not my will but your will be done in my life"? If this scares you, it means that you are taking it seriously. Beyond just saying prayers, you are now pursuing a relationship with God.

In your opinion, what does it mean to align one's life with God's will?

Learning to be a Child of God

Hebrews 5:7-8

In the garden of Gethsemane, Jesus prayed that God would remove the suffering he was about to face. But he then prayed, "…not my will but yours be done." The greatest challenge of prayer is in surrendering your will to God. Even Jesus struggled with it. The writer of Hebrews gives us insight into the life of Jesus. He offered up "prayers and supplications, with loud cries and tears, to him who was able to save him from death, and he was heard because of his reverence" (Hebrews 5:7). Jesus asked the Father to save him from death, and God heard his prayer. In fact, his prayer was answered. Not the request itself, but the statement of surrender, "Nevertheless, not my will but yours be done." In this surrender, Jesus "learned obedience" as God's son through his suffering. Discipleship is about learning to be a child of God. Learning to be his child means learning to surrender your will over to his will.

Key Concepts in this lesson:

♦ When Jesus teaches us how to pray, he provides a model that focuses upon the order and priority of our prayers.

♦ Prayer starts with God and ends with you, and the key is in between—surrendering your will to God.

♦ We must move beyond using prayer mainly for requests to understanding prayer as a conduit for pursuing relationship with God.

Prepare for Next Week's Discussion:
How might you live this out?

In your class or small group, brainstorm some ways to live out this aspect of discipleship. Here are a few ideas to get started:

♦ **Rather than seeking God's hand, seek God's face.**[51] Move away from the "grocery list" type of prayer and simply seek to encounter the glorious beauty of God himself. Center your mind upon God's power, goodness, and love for you.

♦ **Seek God's face by revealing yourself in confession.** Deep relationships are about knowing and being known by another person. Use Psalm 139:1-14 as a guide to reveal your true self to God in a prayer of confession.

♦ **Come face-to-face with God by acknowledging his glory and praising him.** Use Psalm 148 as a guide to reword your own personal prayer of praise.

- **Confess your desire to meet God face-to-face.** Choose an idea from Psalm 51 to form your prayer around. Meet God in your prayer. Examples:

  (1) Confess to God some areas where you are hiding from him.
  (2) What secret are you afraid to face with God and perhaps to others? Confess this to God.
  (3) How is your denial of some sin eating away at your peace of mind? Release this to God.
  (4) Ask God to give you spiritual cleaning.
  (5) Ask God to give you a new spirit and restore the joy of your salvation with him.

Your action plan for this week:

_____

_____

_____

_____

_____

_____

_____

_____

_____

_____

Want to dig deeper on this topic?

A recommended resource:

Timothy Keller. *Prayer: Experiencing Awe and Intimacy with God.* (New York: Dutton, 2014).

Group Check In:

What was your action plan for prayer this week?

How did things go?

What did you learn about God?

What did you learn about yourself?

Notes:

8

GOSPEL

The Spiritual Freedom of Living in Grace

Main Idea: Placing your faith in Jesus is not just how you are saved initially, but it is the center of the Christian's life. Being freed from spiritual slavery, and continually believing the gospel, empowers you to experience real life change.

Bible Passages to Study This Week:

Galatians 1:6-7; 2:4-6
I am astonished that you are so quickly deserting him who called you in the grace of Christ and are turning to a different gospel...

Galatians 5:1-6
For freedom Christ has set us free; stand firm therefore, and do not submit again to a yoke of slavery.

Galatians 5:13-15
For you were called to freedom, brothers. Only do not use your freedom as an opportunity for the flesh, but through love serve one another.

Not Just the ABC's but the A to Z

How would you define the "gospel?" Who needs the gospel?

The gospel of Jesus teaches us that we cannot be saved by our own works of righteousness. We must depend upon God's grace (Romans 3:21-28; Ephesians 2:4-10; Titus 3:4-7). More than simply being the way that we are saved (the A-B-C's), the gospel presents a "fundamental dynamic for living the whole Christian life" (the A to Z).[52] Instead of viewing the gospel as steps (or a stairway) of truths, we should view it as the hub of truth. We must believe the gospel more and more deeply as we live, allowing it to transform every part of our lives. As followers of Jesus we never outgrow or "get beyond" our need for the gospel. Christian living is about aligning your behavior with the gospel (Galatians 2:11-14).

What might it mean to live a "gospel-centered" life?

Distorting the Gospel

Galatians 1:6-7; 2:4-6

Becoming a Christian means you stop trusting in your own works to save you, and you place your trust (faith) in the free gift of God's grace. Most all Christians understand that they were saved by grace. Unfortunately, many Christians think they must work hard to try and stay saved by their works.[53] This is an ancient error that has perpetually plagued Christians. Often referred to as Galatianism, this error teaches that a sinner *becomes* saved by grace, but *stays* saved by works.[54] This view is a distortion of the gospel. When we attempt to mix works and grace into a hybrid gospel, it is not the gospel at all (Galatians 1:6-7). It is spiritual slavery to return to a "works-based salvation" once you have experienced the freedom of salvation by grace (Galatians 2:4-6). Christian religion has frequently been distorted into the false gospel of *"I obey; therefore, I am accepted."* The truth of the gospel says, *"I am accepted through Christ, therefore I obey."*[55]

How do you think you might be tempted to fall into a works-based mentality of salvation?

Stand Firm in Your Freedom
Galatians 5:1-6, 13-15

The gospel of Jesus is vastly different than "religion." Religion makes moral and religious observances the basis of salvation. If your standing before God is dependent upon your performance, you will always be inadequate, feeling anxious and fearful. Trying to be saved by your own moralism or religious observances leads to spiritual slavery. But we have been set free from this in Christ. Paul strongly encourages us to stand firmly in our freedom and not submit again to the burden of work-based salvation. Having been set free from "salvation-by-works-through-law," we must not return to this mentality. We must fully believe Jesus is our Savior and not try to save ourselves by our own works. If we return to this slavery, we are "severed from Christ" and we "fall from grace" (Galatians 5:4). We have been saved by the gospel, so that we might live in line with the gospel.

Paul reminds us that our calling is to "freedom" in Christ (vs. 13). He says (5:1) that we have been set free by salvation by grace, and we must not return to the slavery of thinking we are saved by our works. Jesus' death frees us from the guilt of sin, the penalty of sin, and the power of sin. Jesus said, "And if the Son makes you free, you will be free indeed" (John 8:36). Christianity is not bondage. It is a call to freedom. Yet, some people try to "spy out our freedom" (Galatians 2:4) and make us go back into the slavery of a rule-based religion. But Paul says, "Stand firm," and don't submit to the yoke of slavery! You have been set free in Christ! You are called to freedom!

In what ways might you slip back into spiritual slavery?

Do you find the call to live in freedom to be liberating or intimidating? Why?

Don't Live Like a Prisoner

You can know that you have been set free in Christ, but still live like a prisoner. Some prisoners nostalgically talk about the food they ate in prison and how they actually developed a taste for it. Even out of prison, many still eat like they were still in prison. If you live like a prisoner after you have been set free, you will eventually find yourself back in slavery. Many inmates end up returning to jail because they don't know how to live on the outside.

Paul says it this way, "Only do not use your freedom as an opportunity for the flesh..." (vs. 13b). God did not set us free for us to go out and ruin our lives. So we must not use the freedom Christ has given us as an excuse to live in sinful or selfish behavior. God has set us free that we might know the joys of a beautiful and productive life in his kingdom. God set us free from sin, but he has no intention of giving us freedom to sin.

How might people who live in the freedom of God's grace think, feel and act differently than those "imprisoned" in a false gospel of do's and don'ts?

A Productive Member of the Kingdom

When prisoners are reintroduced back into society, the hope is that the they will become productive members of society. The re-entry movement tries to train former inmates to live in their freedom. This, too, is God's desire, giving us freedom in Christ. His ultimate goal is described in verses 13c-14, "...but through love serve one another. For the whole law is fulfilled in one word: 'You shall love your neighbor as yourself.'"

A main reason prisoners have difficulty adjusting to their freedom is that they are accustomed to someone else telling them every move to make in prison. Unfortunately, many Christians still live in this type of slavery, too. When Christ sets us free, law is replaced with love. The voice of unrelenting code is replaced with the voice of a life giving Spirit (1 Corinthians 15:45; Hebrews 3:6ff). Since you are loved and redeemed, live as a child of light (Ephesians 5:8ff). All of God's instructions and laws were designed to create a new motivating principle in our lives: love for one another. If love and service to our fellow man always dominates our actions, there is no need for any other laws. As Paul says, "the whole law is fulfilled in one word: love." Fighting is a common occurrence in prison. When we live under slavery having to be told every move to make by rules, we end up "biting and devouring one another." Have you ever noticed how much that people in legalistic religion argue and fight, divide and split? You can claim to be a Christian, but still live like a prisoner. When we are always arguing about rules and regulations we become self-absorbed and inward focused. We are not standing in our freedom. Paul says "watch out!" If you live this way you will "consume" each other.

How might legalism prevent you from loving others? How might the gospel free you to really love?

Freedom Transforms You From a Taker to a Giver

When you understand the freedom you have in Christ, it will turn you into a "giver" instead of a "taker." It will make you a servant not a consumer. We often misunderstand freedom to think that freedom means I have certain rights. I have the right to "the pursuit of happiness." I have the right to make sure my spiritual needs are met by the church. It is a mistake to think that Christian freedom means everything is about you. Freedom in Christ means that our hearts have been set free to really love other people and not be enslaved in the prison of our own selfishness. We are set free to breathe the air of living in a community with others. We are empowered to find purpose and joy in serving others while living outside of the walls of selfishness. Freedom in Christ is all about moving from being a consumer to being a contributor. Ironically, it is about moving from being enslaved to being a loving and willing servant. It is about becoming a productive member of kingdom society.

How do you fight a consumeristic mindset?

Key Concepts in this Lesson:

- More than simply the way we are saved, the gospel presents a dynamic for living the whole Christian life.
- We must stand firm in our freedom and not return to a works-based mentality of salvation/living.
- Christianity is not bondage, it is a call to freedom.
- Set free by Christ, we must not live like prisoners but become productive members of the kingdom.

Prepare for Next Week's Discussion:
How might you live this out?

In your class or small group, brainstorm some ways to live out this aspect of discipleship. Here are a few ideas to get started:

- **Live love without restraint.** If you had no fear of being judged, misunderstood, or being taken advantage of, what effect would this have on your relationships? Pick a person (family member, co-worker, friend, etc.) to love this week without restraint. Build the person up, pray for them, and believe in their best motives. Want the exercise to be more impactful? Pick a person you are occasionally at odds with or someone who sees the world differently than you do (cf. Matthew 5:43-48).

- **Be a contributor rather than a consumer.** Often we are quick to identify annoyances and shortcomings of people, businesses, communities, and churches. Instead of lobbying a consumeristic protest, decide to contribute something helpful to a bad situation. Instead of angrily reacting to food coming out late at a restaurant, consider saying to the waitress, *"I see that the restaurant is busy today; thanks for working so hard."* Or instead of complaining that your child's Bible class teacher is never early, volunteer to receive children in class for fifteen minutes prior to class.

♦ **Explore ways you might knowingly or unknowingly be relying on your works to make you right with God.** Ask those who are close to you, whom you trust, to give you feedback on actions, attitudes or beliefs you have exhibited that would lead them to think you are not depending on grace found in Christ quite as much as you would like. Confess these actions/areas to God and ask that the Spirit convince you of Christ's sufficiency and your freedom.

Your action plan for this week:

_____

_____

_____

_____

_____

_____

_____

_____

_____

Want to dig deeper on this topic?
A recommended resource:
Timothy Keller. *Prodigal God: Recovering the Heart of the Christian Faith.* (New York: Riverhead, 2008).

Group Check In:

What was your action plan for gospel this week?

How did things go?

What did you learn about God?

What did you learn about yourself?

Notes:

9

TRAIN

The Disciplines of Being Like Jesus

Main Idea: Being a disciple of Jesus requires training and discipline. Training to be like Jesus starts with your mindset and involves embracing the habits of Jesus into your own life.

Bible Passages to Study This Week:

Matthew 15:10-20
For out of the heart come evil thoughts, murder, adultery, sexual immorality, theft, false witness, slander. These are what defile a person.

Philippians 2:1-11
Do nothing from selfish ambition or conceit, but in humility count others more significant than yourselves. Let each of you look not only to his own interests, but also to the interests of others.

Matthew 14:23
And after he had dismissed the crowds, he went up on the mountain by himself to pray. When evening came, he was there alone....

Spiritual Training

What is the most intense training you have ever been through (athletic, business, etc)?

I played on the basketball team when I was in high school. It was the early 90's and everyone on my team idolized Michael Jordan. We all wore athletic jerseys with "#23" and wore shoes that said "Air Jordan." As teenagers we were glued to the television wondering if Michael Jordan could pull off a "three-peat" (winning 3 consecutive championships). We all wanted to "Be Like Mike." Some guys would wear the shoes and the jerseys but could hardly make a layup. The desire to "be like Mike" was not enough. If you really wanted to be like him, you had to put in the practice, the work, and the training. In the game, you should not expect to have moves like Jordan if you have been unwilling to practice.

We understand the concept of training when it comes to athletics. But what about matters of the spirit? If you want to be like Jesus, you have to put in some heavy spiritual training. It requires focus, intention, and discipline. No one can perform like Christ on the spot. To be like Jesus, we must put in the hours of daily training that no one sees.

What are some habits you have tried to develop to be more like Jesus?

It Starts with Your Thoughts

Matthew 15:10-20

In order to encourage good eating habits, we were told as children "You are what you eat." The things that we put into our bodies ultimately become the building blocks for the way our bodies develop and operate. So we want to make sure we have balanced diets. "Garbage in, garbage out" as they say in the computer industry.

In our spiritual lives, this principle is magnified. Our spiritual development and formation is largely based upon our thought patterns. Evil and dysfunctional behavior start with what is embedded in our "hearts." At the center of our beings is the conscious mind—our thoughts. Training to be like Jesus starts in the battlefield of the mind. The place to start is "taking every thought captive to obey Christ" (2 Corinthians 10:5). You are what you think. As one writer puts it, "The true god of your heart is what your thoughts effortlessly go to when there is nothing else demanding your attention. What do you enjoy daydreaming about? What occupies your mind when you have nothing else to think about?...what do you habitually think about to get joy and comfort in the privacy of your heart?"[56] In reality, every thought "carries a spiritual charge" that either moves you a little closer or a little farther from God.[57]

If you are honest, what does your mind naturally gravitate toward if it is not occupied with anything else? Do your thoughts move you closer or farther away from God?

The Mind of Christ
Philippians 2:1-11

One of the greatest scientific minds of modern times was Albert Einstein. Upon his death, Dr. Thomas S. Harvey removed Einstein's brain and preserved it in formaldehyde for further scientific study.[58] Scientists wanted to look into the mind of Einstein and see what made him so wise. What if we could look into the mind of Christ? What would we see there? We are not left to speculation. When we look into the mind of Christ we see humility and self-sacrifice. Scripture encourages us to reproduce the mind of Christ in our own thoughts and *"in humility count others more significant than yourselves…look not only to your own interests, but also to the interests of others"* (Philippians 2:3-4). When we look into the mind of Christ, we see that his thoughts were focused on obeying his heavenly Father and serving others. Training to be like Jesus begins with repentance and self-denial. When you truly submit your life to God's will, humility floods your life. Jesus surrendered himself to God's will to be a sacrifice for humanity. As a result, his mindset was characterized by great humility. To be like Christ, we must surrender to God's will, which will bring about a humility of life and self-sacrifice for the interests of others.

Share a time when there was a radical change in your mindset. How did the change come about? What difference did it make in your life?

The Habits of Jesus
Matthew 14:23

Jesus was not just a philosopher speaking wise sayings or a peddler of theological theory. Jesus was the embodiment of his teaching. He was the word of God in the flesh; he embodied the truth of God that provides real life. Jesus told his followers, *"I gave you an example that you should do as I did to you"* (John 13:15). The Bible encourages us to *"follow in his steps"* (1 Peter 2:21). When we look carefully at the life of Jesus, we see observable patterns of behavior. Jesus had certain habits that characterized his life. As disciples training to be like our Master, we should adopt these behaviors into the regular routines of our lives. The following is not an exhaustive list, but here are five habits we see Jesus embracing in his life:

1. ***Regular Quiet Times*** (Matthew 14:23; cf. Mark 1:35; Luke 4:42). Throughout his ministry, Jesus would go into solitude away from the noise and busyness of life. He regularly had quiet times alone with God. Times of quiet and stillness are an important discipline that should be prioritized in our lives if we want to train to think and live like Jesus.

2. ***Bathed in Prayer*** Jesus was devoted and consistent in his prayer life. Throughout the gospels, we see that Jesus made conversation with God a priority. His prayers were heartfelt (John 17), sometimes by himself (Luke 5:16), sometimes with others (Luke 9:28), intimate in conversation (Luke 11:1ff; calling God "Father"), and always according to God's will (Luke 22:42). Jesus conversed with God in the midst of the daily circumstances of life (John 11:41-42) but also dedicated long time periods for focused prayer (Luke 6:12). To train to be like Jesus, the discipline of prayer must be a top priority.

3. ***Immersed in the Word*** Jesus was thoroughly familiar with Scripture (Luke 4:16-21). In moments of temptation, he relied upon his memorization of the Word (Matthew 4:1-11). Beyond just knowing Scripture, Jesus lived scripture. Jesus was the Word of God in the flesh (John 1:1-14). Knowledge of the Bible alone can make you arrogant (cf. 1 Corinthians 8:1; John 5:39-42). Spiritual growth and training comes from Bible application. Jesus trains his disciples to both know the will of God and to do it (Matthew 7:21-23).

4. ***Devoted to Worship*** Even though Jesus is the Son of God, worshipping the Father was a priority in his life. He surrendered to the Father's will and gave him praise. Concluding the Lord's Supper, Jesus sang a song of praise with his apostles (Matthew 26:30; Mark 14:26). Jesus had the custom of meeting with others for study and worship in the synagogue (Luke 4:16). Even now, Jesus is committed to participating in communal worship in the church (Hebrews 2:12). To be like Jesus, we should cultivate the discipline of private worship to God, and commit to worshipping regularly with other believers.

5. ***Focused on Relationships*** Some religions teach that real spirituality is a personal, isolated event. Even some Christians seem to think that their spiritual walk is only between them and God. But Jesus focused on the importance of relationships. He cultivated deep personal relationships with a spiritual focus. He chose twelve Apostles, had an inner circle of three disciples (Peter, James, John), and had rich spiritual friendships (Lazarus, Mary, Martha) (John 11:5). The gospels are full of Jesus' deep conversations with his closest friends. Being like Jesus, we must invest in spiritual relationships. Growing as a disciple means we need spiritually minded friends to whom we can confess and with whom we pray (cf. James 5:16).

From your study, what other habits do you see Jesus cultivating that we should imitate?

Key Concepts in this lesson:

- ◆ Becoming like Jesus requires heavy spiritual training involving focus, intention, and discipline.
- ◆ Your spiritual development and formation is largely based upon your thought patterns. Training to be like Jesus starts in the battlefield of the mind.
- ◆ As disciples training to be like our Master, we should adopt the observable habits that characterized his life into the regular routines of our lives.

<u>**Prepare for Next Week's Discussion:**</u>
How might you live this out?

In your class or small group, brainstorm some ways to live out this aspect of discipleship. Here are a few ideas to get started:

- ◆ **Engage in a thought detox for the week.** Make a commitment to purge your mind of toxic thoughts this week. Reject negative thinking, worry, anxiety, bitterness and impure thoughts. Discipline your thinking this week and take every thought captive for Christ.

- ◆ **Choose one of the habits of Jesus and devote yourself to it this week.** For the next seven days intentionally adopt one of the habits of Jesus and center your life around that activity. Consider it an "intensive" week for the development of one of Jesus' habits into your life.

♦ **Engage in a research project of the gospels and make a list of the habits of Jesus' life.** After listing the observable habits of Jesus' life, create a plan for the next 3 months where you will choose one of his habits to focus on each week.

Your action plan for this week:

_____

_____

_____

_____

_____

_____

_____

_____

_____

_____

_____

Want to dig deeper on this topic?
A recommended resource:
Richard Foster. *The Celebration of Discipline: The Path to Spiritual Growth.* 3rd ed. (San Francisco: HarperCollins, 1998).

Group Check In:

What was your action plan for training this week?

How did things go?

What did you learn about God?

What did you learn about yourself?

Notes:

10

IDOLS

Identifying the Real Affections of Your Heart

Main Idea: At the heart of discipleship is making Christ the real affection of your heart. To fully follow Jesus, we must identify the idols of our hearts, dismantle them and replace them with the beauty of Christ.

Bible Passages to Study This Week:

Romans 7:7-11
For sin, seizing an opportunity through the commandment, deceived me and through it killed me.

Exodus 20:1-6
You shall have no other gods before me.

Romans 8:12-14
For if you live according to the flesh you will die, but if by the Spirit you put to death the deeds of the body, you will live.

Hebrews 12:1-2
...let us lay aside every weight, and sin which clings so closely, and let us run with endurance the race that is set before us, looking to Jesus...."

The Heart Behind Disobedience
Romans 7:7-11

When in your life have been most tempted to be rebellious?

Why do we break the law? Why do we find ourselves desiring what is forbidden? Why do we find what is off-limits to be so enticing? The Apostle Paul explains that something about rules actually stirs up a desire to want to break them (Romans 7:7-11). For example, few may think of breaking a window until a sign is placed on it reading, "Do Not Break This Window." The presence of the law actually makes us want to break it. More rules do not stop the desire for disobedience; actually, more rules kindle the fires of disobedience within the heart. The heart is not changed by more rules. More than moral restraint of the will, we need a complete transformation of heart. The desire for disobedience must be withered within our hearts.

Why do you think law actually stirs a desire within us to be lawbreakers?

Identify Your Idols

Exodus 20:1-6

When God gave his top ten commandments, he started with two commandments against idolatry. God said, "Have no other gods before me" and do not "construct any image" to bow down before (Exodus 20:3-4). Martin Luther observed that anytime you break commandments 2-10 you have already broken the first commandment.[59] The underlying cause behind all sin is idolatry—making something else your god. Behind any particular sin is your heart's failure to trust God and making something in life more important than him (cf. Genesis 3:5). Anything in life can become an idol to your heart. An idol has been defined as "anything more important to you than God, anything that absorbs your heart and imagination more than God, anything you seek to give you what only God can give."[60] If you want to really be a disciple of Jesus, it starts with the deep affections of your heart. You must start by identifying your idols. Dismantling the idols of your heart is at the core of discipleship. It is not only "bad" things that become idols. The most dangerous idols are good things that have become *ultimate* in our lives. Discipleship begins with not having any other gods before the true God.

What good thing in your life has the most potential to be an idol for you?

Dismantling Your Idols

Romans 8:12-14

What is sin?   J.I. Packer defines sin as "ungodly and anti-God inclinations in the heart."[61]   Jesus defines discipleship as "taking up your cross daily" (Luke 9:23). The cross was an instrument of death. Following Jesus means that we must see the ugliness of our personal sin. John Owen once wrote, "Be killing sin, or sin will be killing you."[62] We must see the seriousness of sin in our lives and have a desire to put sin to death. But we cannot overcome sin by our own efforts and desire alone. We must acknowledge our need for God's help, and embrace the spiritual strength he provides to demolish our idols. God provides divine power to bring down strongholds in our lives (2 Corinthians 10:4). Paul speaks directly to this in Romans 8:13, *"For if you live according to the flesh you will die, but if by the Spirit you put to death the deeds of the body, you will live."* The only way we can put sin to death in our lives is by tapping into the power of the Spirit. One of the primary works of the Spirit is conviction within the heart. We must open ourselves up to this leading and not quench his conviction upon us.

How have your own attempts at holy-living fallen flat?

Getting to the Root of Your Heart's Affection

If you try to deal with sins by your flesh, they will keep coming back. There is a big difference in trying to morally restrain your heart and having a heart that is supernaturally changed.[63] Instead of trying to deal with the symptoms (behaviors of sin) you must get to the root of your sin. The root of sin is what makes it attractive to you. The desire for sin must be withered at the motivational level within our hearts. We must ask the deeper questions of why the sin is attractive to our hearts. We must get at the sin beneath the sin. For example, why do we steal?

Ultimately it is because we lack a trust in God's provision. Why do we commit adultery? Is it not because we think the arms of a lover can provide a deeper intimacy that we don't trust God can deliver? Sins of the heart, the idols we serve, are ultimately the result of failing to believe and trust God. Something else in life is functioning as your "savior." To get to the root of sin and dismantle your idols, you must replace the affections of your heart with an affection for Christ. When we follow the Spirit's lead, we will see that he always shines light on the beauty of Christ. He kindles affection for Christ within our hearts. When we set our minds on the things of the Spirit, he will make Jesus real in our hearts. As the affection of Christ grows stronger in our hearts, all other affections are withered within.

What do you find most appealing about Jesus that withers the attractiveness of sin?

Replacing Your Idols

Hebrews 12:1-2

Discipleship is all about taking up the cross of self-denial and following Jesus. We must put to death sin's affection in our hearts by the Spirit. The Spirit helps us do this, when we allow him, by showing us the beauty of Christ. Dallas Willard explains it this way: "The process of spiritual formation in Christ is one of progressively replacing...destructive images and ideas with the images and ideas that filled the mind of Jesus himself."[64] The pathway to spiritual life always involves two things: (1) putting your sins to death by the Spirit and (2) filling your mind with the great things Christ has done for you.[65] This is something that must always be done, because sin always indwells within us.[66] We must "daily" take up the cross of killing sin, and focus on the beauty of following Jesus. Every day we must decide to once again identify and kill the sin that "clings so closely," and "look to Jesus" and his beauty (Hebrews 12:1-2). Idols are only dismantled when they are identified and replaced with a superior affection within the heart. Seeing the love of God and the beauty of Christ sharply is what will wither the root of sin in our hearts. As Timothy Keller says, *"Fear-based repentance makes us hate ourselves. Joy-based repentance makes us hate the sin."* We must "taste and see the Lord is good" (Psalm 34:8). We must "rejoice in the Lord always" (Philippians 4:4). Idols are brought down when Jesus becomes real in our hearts.

What are some ways that Jesus has become "real" to your heart?

Key Concepts in this lesson:

- More than moral restraint of the will, we need a complete transformation of heart. The desire for disobedience must be withered within our hearts.
- The underlying cause behind all sin is idolatry—making something else your god.
- The desire for sin must be withered at the motivational level within the heart.
- Idols are only dismantled when they are identified and replaced with a superior affection within the heart.

Prepare for Next Week's Discussion:
How might you live this out?

In your class or small group, brainstorm some ways to live out this aspect of discipleship. Here are a few ideas to get started:

- **Intently work on *identifying* the idols of your life.** This week focus on prayer and meditation asking God to help you see what things in your life you have made more ultimate than him. Before idols can be dismantled in your heart, they must be identified.

- **Intently work on *dismantling* the idols in your life.** Pray and ask God to drain the life out of your sin. Be specific to God; he can take it. Ask the Holy Spirit to help you become more aware of your sinful habits. Ask him to make God's love for you more real in your heart.

- **Spend time this week rejoicing in Jesus.** Identify the things about Jesus that you find beautiful. Make a list. Focus on these things this week. Kindle the fires of affection in your heart for Jesus through intense sessions of private worship and prayer.

Your action plan for this week:

_____

_____

_____

_____

_____

_____

_____

_____

_____

_____

_____

Want to dig deeper on this topic?

A recommended resource:

Timothy Keller. *Counterfeit Gods.* (New York: Riverhead, 2009).

Group Check In:

What was your action plan for idols this week?

How did things go?

What did you learn about God?

What did you learn about yourself?

11

APPLY

The Importance of Bible Living

Main Idea: Spiritual maturity goes beyond just knowing the Bible to actually applying the Bible into your life. Discipleship centers upon being receptive to the Spirit's transformative work to change your life into the image of Christ.

Bible Passages to Study This Week:

Matthew 13:13-15
Though seeing, they do not see; though hearing, they do not hear or understand.

1 Corinthians 8:1
We know that, "We all possess knowledge." But knowledge puffs up while love builds up.

James 1:22-25
But be doers of the word, and not hearers only.

2 Corinthians 13:5
Examine yourselves, to see whether you are in the faith. Test yourselves.

Having Ears that Don't Hear

Matthew 13:13-15

What is the difference in hearing someone and actually listening to them?

God has given many wonderful gifts to humanity. Unfortunately, in our fallen world many of these pure gifts have been misused and tainted. Adultery is the corruption of God's gift of sex. Gluttony is the corruption of God's gift of food. Laziness is the corruption of rest.

Even the gift of God's Word can be corrupted. The prophet Isaiah and Jesus both warned of religious people who are always hearing spiritual truth but don't really "hear" it (Isaiah 6:9-10; Matthew 13:14-15). It is an extremely dangerous thing to study God's word but not let it impact and change your life. It is not enough to simply hear the truth with your mind; you must be willing to allow your heart to hear it too.

The correct motivation for studying the Bible should be love. First, it should be our love for God and desire to know him better personally. Secondly, it should be our desire to lovingly communicate these personally applied truths to other people (cf. Matthew 23:1-7).

We must be cautious as we gain knowledge of the Bible. It is possible to worship the Bible without worshipping God. Bibliolatry is worshipping the Bible as an idol. We need to study the "word of the Lord" so we can come to know and love the "Lord of the word." Ultimately, good Bible study and interpretation has personal, spiritual transformation as its destination. What value is the Bible if it does not change us more into God's image and bring us closer to him?

What is involved in moving a truth from being a mere fact to being something that you actually take to heart?

The Danger of Bible Knowledge
1 Corinthians 8:1

During Jesus' life, the Pharisees knew the Bible (Old Testament) better than anyone.[67] Yet, they were the very ones responsible for crucifying him. They knew all the prophecies about the Messiah. They looked right in his eyes. They quoted the Old Testament the entire time. And they missed him. Knowledge is a powerful ally, but it can also be a dangerous weapon. Paul warns about the danger of knowledge making a person arrogant (1 Corinthians 8:1). We should all honestly ask ourselves why we study the Bible. What is my motivation for reading and studying the Bible? We must guard against simply gathering facts and accumulating knowledge. Such an approach will only make you arrogant and worthless to God's kingdom purposes. Before any other reason, our foremost purpose for studying the Bible should be for our own personal spiritual growth and transformation. We must turn from knowing *about* God to a personal knowledge *of* God.[68]

What have been your motivations for studying the Bible?

Real Spiritual Maturity: Bible Application

James 1:22-25

What is the basis of real spiritual maturity? Spiritual maturity is not just about how much you know. Rather, it is based upon how much you have embraced the truth you know into your life. Andy Stanley has pointed out, *"Spiritual maturity is not synonymous with Bible knowledge. Spiritual maturity is synonymous with Bible application."*[69] The truthfulness of this statement is clear in James 1:22-25.

James tells us that we deceive ourselves if we merely listen to God's word without doing what it says. He compares it to looking in a mirror, seeing yourself in disarray, and then doing nothing about it. No one gets credit for looking in the mirror. You get credit for looking in the mirror and doing something about what you see there. You are *not* blessed for what you know; you are blessed by "doing" (vs. 25). It is not enough to know the Bible; we must live the Bible. Certainly, you cannot apply the truth of the Bible if you don't know it. But the key is not just knowing truth but applying it. "Doing the Bible" is the real mark of spiritual maturity.

In your opinion, is it more difficult to know the Bible or to live the Bible?

The Importance of Introspection
2 Corinthians 13:5

As a parent who sees your children daily, you may not notice how much they grow over a period of months. But if a grandparent sees your children for the first time in months, they will usually shout, *"My, how much you have grown!"* It certainly gives God tremendous joy to see spiritual growth in each one of us. But spiritual growth only occurs when we practice self-examination (introspection) and make changes that result in personal development.

When Martin Luther ignited the Protestant Reformation by nailing his *95 Theses* to the door of the church in Germany, the first on his list was essentially, *"All of life is repentance."* To be a disciple of Jesus means that we follow his manner of life. Discipleship is a continual process of change, growth, development and transformation into the image of Christ. Taking up the daily cross of discipleship means that we continually repent of attitudes and actions that are contrary to the Jesus-life.

Up to this point in your life, how serious have you been about personal introspection and character development?

The Spirit's Work of Transformation
2 Corinthians 3:17-18

Spiritual transformation is the work of the Holy Spirit. The Lord, who is the Spirit, is in the business of changing us into the image of Christ. The purpose of daily repentance is *not* to earn God's favor. Rather, because we have been saved by grace, the purpose of a life of repentance is to continually connect with the joy of being united with Christ. With that constant connection, evil desires are weakened to do anything that is contrary to the heart of God.[70] Like a surgeon using a scalpel, the Holy Spirit uses the Word of God to convict our hearts and remove destructive attitudes and behaviors (Hebrews 4:12). When we are convicted by the Word to make changes in our lives, we must not quench the holy impulse upon our hearts (1 Thessalonians 5:19). We must be open to the Spirit's leading (Romans 8:14). Discipleship is a continual call to bring forth the fruit of repentance in our lives (Matthew 3:8). Some people live as if they are immovable and enslaved to spiritually dysfunctional behaviors. But anyone can change with the help of God's Spirit. In order for this to happen, we must not resist his work in our hearts (Acts 7:51).

What area of your life do you want to target for spiritual growth over the next year? Share yours with the group and pray for one another.

Asking for Help

One of the best ways to apply the Bible to your life is to ask for honest feedback from your closest friends. Christians are to admonish, encourage, and help one another in spiritual growth. We are to confess our sins to each other and pray for one another (James 5:16). Some of the most damaging spiritual behaviors are almost impossible to see in ourselves but are clear to others around us (i.e. pride, selfishness, etc.). One of the best ways to grow spiritually is to find another respected and trustworthy Christian and ask for constructive spiritual feedback. Ask your friend, "What behaviors do you see in me that are most unlike Jesus?" Give your friend permission to be honest, and assure them that you are trying to identify a specific area of your life to focus upon for spiritual growth.

How do you feel about asking for spiritual feedback from a friend?

Key Concepts in this lesson:

- ◆ Before any other reason, our foremost purpose for studying the Bible should be for our own personal spiritual growth and transformation.

- ◆ "Doing the Bible" (Bible application) is the real mark of spiritual maturity.

- ◆ Spiritual growth only occurs when we practice self-examination (introspection) and make changes that result in personal development.

- ◆ Spiritual transformation is the work of the Holy Spirit who is in the business of changing us into the image of Christ.

Prepare for Next Week's Discussion:
How might you live this out?

In your class or small group, brainstorm some ways to live out this aspect of discipleship. Here are a few ideas to get started:

- ◆ **Ask one of your closest spiritually-minded friends for constructive feedback.** Assure your friend that you want honest suggestions of a specific area where you need to further develop into Christlikeness. Swallow your pride and accept the advice. Then develop an intentional plan to study the Bible's instruction in this area, and apply it to your life.

- ◆ **Identify a Bible teaching that you have consistently neglected or have not developed in your life.** It might be something like helping the sick (Matthew 25:39-40), caring for widows and orphans (James 1:27), or sharing your faith through personal evangelism (Matthew 4:19). Whatever the area, commit to going on a personal crusade to apply this teaching to your life.

♦ **Read a selected section of Scripture this week asking, "What change is God calling me to make in my life?"** You might focus your study on the Sermon on the Mount (Matthew 5-7). Read slowly and deliberately. Pray after each section and ask God to give insight into a specific way that you need to "live" this teaching. Take notes of your study in a journal and log your spiritual progress.

Your action plan for this week:

_____

_____

_____

_____

_____

_____

_____

_____

_____

_____

Want to dig deeper on this topic?

A recommended resource:
Charles M. Sheldon. *In His Steps.* (Grand Rapids: Baker, 1984).

Group Check In:

What was your action plan for "apply" this week?

How did things go?

What did you learn about God?

What did you learn about yourself?

Notes:

12

SPIRIT

<u>The Spirit-Filled, Spirit-Led Life</u>

Main Idea: Being led by the Spirit means that you follow his direction and guidance for your life. Being filled by the Spirit is a relational concept of being deeply connected with God in your life.

Bible Passages to Study This Week:

Romans 8:12-13
For all who are led by the Spirit of God are sons of God.

Ephesians 5:18-21
And do not get drunk with wine, for that is debauchery, but be filled with the Spirit....

Galatians 5:16-25
If we live by the Spirit, let us also keep in step with the Spirit.

1 Corinthians 6:15-20
But he who is joined to the Lord becomes one spirit with him...Or do you not know that your body is a temple of the Holy Spirit within you, whom you have from God?

The Greatest Influence Over You

<u>Romans 8:12-13</u>

What person has had the greatest influence upon your life?

The people around us have tremendous influence upon us. Parents, teachers, and friends all greatly impact our lives either for good or bad. The interactions we have with others leave tremendous impressions upon us. Rather than being motivated by popular opinion or unduly swayed by others (Matthew 22:16), Jesus followed the leading of the Spirit (John 3:34; Luke 4:1). As the perfect Son of God, Jesus followed the Spirit's direction. As disciples of Jesus and children of God, we too must follow the Spirit's lead. In our lives we hear many voices that are all clamoring for us to follow their leading. But as a disciple, we follow the voice and leading of the Spirit.

Currently, what is the loudest voice in your life?

- The voice in my own head
- The voice of peers
- The voice of a mentor
- The voice of other's expectations
- The voice of God's truth
- Other

Filled with a Person

Ephesians 5:18-21

Scripture directs us to "be filled with the Spirit." This is something we are commanded to continually do, yet it is not something we can totally control. The passage is essentially telling us to "continually allow yourselves to be filled with the Spirit." We must position our hearts to receive, surrender to, and welcome the cooperation of the Spirit in our lives.

But being filled with the Spirit is not like being charged with an impersonal, spiritual force. The Holy Spirit is a person. To be filled with the Spirit is to be filled with a person. It has everything to do with cultivating a relationship. Being filled with a person is about constantly being aware of their presence and hanging on their every word. When we are filled with a person, we are under their influence. When you are underneath the influence of a person, you are extremely motivated to please them and listen to their advice.

In your experience, what things most cultivate deep relationships? How might this relate to being filled with the Spirit of God?

Live by the Spirit

Galatians 5:16-25

Being led by the Spirit's influence requires a willingness to live by the Spirit's direction. We must choose to take steps in life that are in alignment with the steps of the Spirit. The Spirit illuminates reality, reveals truth, and provides direction for life. Being filled with the Spirit means we are filled with the Word (compare Ephesians 5:19 and Colossians 3:16). To be saturated with the Spirit means we are saturated with the truth about reality. Reality is revealed in his Word. Being directed by the influence of the Spirit means that we seek to please him (not grieve him; Ephesians 4:30), and we listen to his direction (and don't quench his direction; 1 Thessalonians 5:19). If you are convicted by a truth in the Bible but don't allow that truth to change your life, you have rejected the Spirit's influence. You are quenching the Spirit. As your mind is informed through studying the Word, the Spirit works to convict your heart and conscience to live in harmony with his truth (cf. Romans 9:1). Living by the Spirit means that you follow the influence of the Spirit's leading in your life.

What things most prevent you from following the Spirit's influence?

Filled with Relationship
1 Corinthians 6:16-20

Being filled with the person of the Spirit means we welcome a constant sense of connection with God in our hearts. At baptism, believers receive the gift of the Holy Spirit (Acts 2:38). We have the Holy Spirit dwelling within our bodies as a gift. The Spirit of God longs for a deep, intimate relationship with you (James 4:5). God wants to draw near to you in a personal relationship (James 4:8). Using the analogy of the union of marriage, God makes clear that he wants to be joined with you and become one spirit with you (1 Cor. 6:17). This deep connection is called "fellowship of the Spirit" (2 Corinthians 13:14). Being filled with the Spirit is a relational concept. God wants to be close to you. Are you allowing your heart to be led close to him?

How do you feel about having a deep relationship with God? Is it appealing or intimidating to you?

Relational Closeness

What makes you feel close to another person? Scripture compares relational closeness to God to the intimacy of marriage. Several principles of relational intimacy that are true for close friendships and especially marriage can help us draw near to God.

First, speaking openly. Relational closeness is a desire to bare your heart to another person, to be vulnerable and accepted by them. In your relationship with God this comes through prayer. This is "face to face" time with God. Consider Psalm 27:8 which says, "Seek his face! Your face, Lord, I will seek."

Second, hearing actively. To be filled with God, we must hear him. Are we actively listening to God? Active listening is about being a "doer" of the word. Do we show hearts that are open to his word? Are we introspective and receptive to the direction of God?

Third, desiring passionately. We feel close to someone who spends time thinking of us and shows that we are important to them. God wants us to "seek" him. To be close to God, we must desire him for who he is. Rather than wanting what God provides, we must simply desire him for who he is.

Which principle of relational closeness is one that you most need to cultivate in your closeness with God?

Key Concepts in this lesson:

♦ In our lives we hear many voices that are all clamoring for us to follow their leading, but disciples choose to follow the voice and leading of the Spirit.

♦ Being filled with the Spirit is to be filled with a person and has everything to do with cultivating a relationship.

♦ As your mind is informed through studying the Word, the Spirit works to convict your heart and conscience to live in harmony with his truth.

♦ Being filled with the person of the Spirit means we welcome a constant sense of connection with God in our hearts.

Prepare for Next Week's Discussion:
How might you live this out?

In your class or small group, brainstorm some ways to live out this aspect of discipleship. Here are a few ideas to get started:

♦ **Honestly evaluate your personal relationship with God.** How close do you feel to God in your life currently? Do you feel deeply connected or relationally distant? For the next week, keep a spiritual journal. Write down things that you do every day to help cultivate your relationship with God.

♦ **Choose one of the principles of relational closeness to focus upon this week.** Which of the three principles (speak openly, hear actively, or desire passionately) most needs development in your life? Choose one and focus your time on it this week. You might focus on prayer, Bible study and application, or cultivating your heart's desire for God.

♦ **Brainstorm the greatest barriers in your life to being filled with the Spirit.** Make a list of the things that distract you most from being filled with the person of the Spirit. Make a commitment to eliminate the top thing on your list this week.

Your action plan for this week:

_____

_____

_____

_____

_____

_____

_____

_____

_____

_____

_____

_____

Want to dig deeper on this topic?

A recommended resource:

Francis Chan. *Forgotten God: Reversing Our Tragic Neglect of the Holy Spirit.* (Colorado Springs: David C. Cook, 2009).

Group Check In:

What was your action plan for "Spirit" this week?

How did things go?

What did you learn about God?

What did you learn about yourself?

13

SHARE

The Jesus-Life is Contagious

Main Idea: The message of Jesus is one that is to be shared. In order to be effective in sharing the Jesus-life, we must be authentic in our faith, relationally close to those who need Jesus, and clear in our communication of why Jesus makes a difference in our lives.

Bible Passages to Study This Week:

Matthew 4:18-22
Follow me, and I will make you fishers of men.

Matthew 5:13-16
You are the salt of the earth...You are the light of the world.

I Peter 3:14-17
...always being prepared to make a defense to anyone who asks you for a reason for the hope that is in you.

A Message to Be Shared
Matthew 4:18-22

What is something in your life that you could not keep to yourself?

Maybe for you it was a great movie. It could have been a new product you just used and loved. For many of us it is the birth of a child or new grandchildren. We all have had the experience of discovering something that had such an impact on us that we can't help but share it with others. Some things are so great that we just can't keep it to ourselves.

The message of the gospel is a message meant to be shared. It is "good news," the best news of all. We can be saved by placing our faith in the free gift of God's grace through Christ. It is there that we can find wholeness, meaning, and fullness of life. Rather than spending our lives in idle pursuits, the most meaningful thing you can do is share the gospel of grace with others. Part of the very definition of what it means to be a follower of Jesus is that you are made to be a "fisher of people," sharing your faith in Christ with others. Like fish being drawn to a lure, there should be something that attracts people to Christ through your life.

What are some characteristics that draw you to certain people instead of others?

Authentic Enough

Matthew 5:13

Jesus says that his followers should be like salt to the world. This imagery is chosen by Jesus to demonstrate the type of impact we should have upon others around us. In the book, *Becoming a Contagious Christian,* the authors identify three primary uses of salt across human history which may give us an indication as to why Jesus chose this metaphor:

1. *Salt makes us thirsty.* Salt stimulates thirst. Authentic disciples demonstrate a sense of purpose, an inner peace and joy that creates a spiritual thirst in the people around them.

2. *Salt spices things up.* When something tastes bland, we reach for salt to enhance the flavor. When Christians live out their faith authentically and boldly, they put a zing into a sometimes bland cup of soup. Christians challenge people with apparent radical points of view. Christians put spice in the lives of those around them.

3. *Salt preserves.* Salt was once used to prevent foods from spoiling. Christ-honoring people hold back the moral decay of society. God uses his people to hold back the tidal wave of evil that threatens to sweep the land.

Jesus makes clear that salt is only useful when it is potent in its "saltiness." If salt loses its authentic salty taste, then it is useless. If we are going to share our faith with others, we must fully embrace it ourselves first. In order to have any impact on others, we must first be authentic in our discipleship. You cannot share what you don't have yourself. You might have lots of non-Christian friends with whom you can share your faith, but if they see hypocrisy in your life you will have no effect upon them. Salt that has lost its flavor is worthless.

What is the "saltiest" thing about your Christian life? What are the aspects of your life that have perhaps lost their "saltiness?"

Close Enough

Matthew 5:13

You can have the most highly flavored salt in the world, but it will not produce any results unless it is in contact with food. For salt to have impact upon food, it has to be close enough to whatever it is supposed to affect. It is not enough to be an authentic believer in Jesus. We must get close to other people who need him in order to share our faith. It is easy to become "so religious" that you actually alienate yourself from those who need Jesus. In order to share the Jesus-life, we must not only be authentically living it ourselves, but we must also cultivate spiritual friendships with those who don't know Jesus. Jesus never intended for us to be isolated from the world. For salt to have an effect, it must be in contact. We must have interaction with people who need Jesus if we are going to be "salt."

Who in your life might you have the most influence upon?

Clear Enough

Matthew 5:14-16

The Italian, Christian leader Saint Francis of Assisi (1182-1226 A.D.) once wrote, "Preach the gospel, and when necessary use words." He was emphasizing the importance of being "salt" by being an example of the Christian life to unbelievers. But to have the most impact in sharing the Jesus-life with others, we must also be "light" to them.

What does light do? The most basic answer is that light makes things visible and helps us see things for what they really are. That's what we mean when we say we want to "shed some light" on an issue. The central idea of being "light" is clearly and attractively presenting God's truth to others. It means to illuminate in order to show what Christianity really is. To be "light to the world" means that we clearly articulate the content of the gospel message in an understandable way to others (cf. 2 Corinthians 4:5-6). Jesus wants his followers not only to be an example by living out his teachings but also to be active in explaining his message of forgiveness and grace with precision and accuracy.

What is one of the biggest "light bulb moments" you have had in your faith journey? How might you share this in a clear way with others?

Contagious Living

1 Peter 3:14-17

Usually when we think of something being contagious, we think about sickness. But good things in life can be contagious as well. Have you ever been around someone with a contagious laugh? When he or she starts laughing, you can't help but join! The transformed life infused in us through the Spirit by living the Christ-centered life should be contagious as well. Imagine seeing a person who exudes love, joy and peace in their demeanor and actions despite bad circumstances. Who doesn't want that kind of life? When fully embraced, the Jesus-life is contagious.

The Apostle Peter encourages us to always be prepared to explain to others the "reason for the hope that is in you." The life of the disciple is one of transparency and courage. We must "go public" with our faith. The character of the disciple should be such that others naturally question why we have such peace and hope even in the midst of sometimes suffering for our faith. Authentic lives of discipleship are a catalyst for questions which create opportunity for sharing our testimony of faith. The life of the disciple is radically different than the lives of others. We are to live as lights in the darkness, doing good for those around us. When we are sacrificial in doing good to all people, whether they believe our message or not, they must hear the message of the gospel to even make sense of our lives.[71] In the moment when the questions about our faith come, we must be prepared to answer.

If someone asked you, "Why are you a Christian?" how would you answer?

Key Concepts in this Lesson:

♦ Part of the definition of a disciple of Jesus is being a "fisher of people" by sharing your faith in Christ with others.

♦ If we are going to share our faith with others, we must first fully embrace it ourselves. In order to have any impact on others, we must first be authentic in our discipleship.

♦ In order to share the Jesus-life, we must cultivate spiritual friendships with those who don't know Jesus.

♦ To be "light to the world" means that we clearly articulate the content of the gospel message in an understandable way to others.

Prepare for Next Week's Discussion:

How might you live this out?

In your class or small group, brainstorm some ways to live out this aspect of discipleship. Here are a few ideas to get started:

♦ **Make a list of people you personally know that need Jesus.** Spend time praying for these people individually and asking God to give you the courage and opportunity to share your faith with them. Be vigilant to the doors God opens, and have courage to walk through them this week.

♦ **Honestly evaluate your authenticity as a disciple of Jesus.** What are the areas of your life that most make you vulnerable to the accusation of hypocrisy in your faith? Work hard this week to evaluate how *potent* you are in your influence for Christ. Repent of those areas where you are inauthentic in your faith.

♦ **Start going to the same places to build relationships with unbelievers.** Go to the same restaurant and ask for the same server, frequent the same coffee shop and visit with the same barista or look for the same cashier at the grocery store. Find ways to come into *close proximity* with people who need Jesus. Be authentic about your faith as you invest in building a relationship.

Your action plan for this week:

_____

_____

_____

_____

_____

_____

_____

_____

_____

_____

_____

Want to dig deeper on this topic?

A recommended resource:

Bill Hybels and Mark Mittelberg. ***Becoming a Contagious Christian.*** (Grand Rapids: Zondervan, 1996).

Group Check In:

What was your action plan for "share" this week?

How did things go?

What did you learn about God?

What did you learn about yourself?

Notes:

Part 3: Beyond

40 Days of Daily Discipleship

Welcome to BEYOND:
40 Days of Daily Discipleship

"For you have been called for this purpose, since Christ also suffered for you, leaving you an example for you to follow in His steps"
−1 Peter 2:21

You may have just been baptized into Christ and are now a new follower of Jesus. Or, you may have been a disciple of Jesus for many years, but you want to strengthen your relationship with God.

This section is designed to guide you as you continue to develop your faith. The hope is that you will follow a daily routine of study and meditation upon God's word for the next forty days.

After Jesus was baptized by John in the Jordan River, immediately he went into the wilderness, presumably to meditate upon his mission. For forty days he was there fasting and praying. During this time he was tempted by the Devil (Matthew 4:1-11). If you are a new disciple of Jesus, recently baptized, you may find yourself tempted by Satan to leave your newfound faith. This is why it is important to begin your new life following spiritual routines that will discipline your heart and mind to remain spiritually focused.

On the next few pages, you will be guided into daily studies of God's Word. Hopefully, this forty-day regimen will develop into a daily habit for you that will continue for the rest of your journey as a disciple of Jesus Christ.

"Your word I have treasured in my heart, that I may not sin against You" −Psalm 119:11

Week 1
Intimacy with God

This week you will study how to experience an intimate relationship with God. God's main message in the Bible is that he wants a close relationship with you. In this study you will learn that you can feel close to God in your daily walk with Him.

Day 1
God Can Be Experienced in Your Life

Read <u>Acts 17:16-34</u> several times and study this passage. Although Paul was very educated in the Hebrew Scriptures, he does not use Scripture to show the "unknown God" to this audience. What facts does Paul choose to focus upon to teach this audience (who believed in many gods and knew nothing of the Hebrew Scriptures) about the one, true God?

Paul compliments this audience for being "very religious" (vs. 22, NASB). Not only were they religious, but they were worshippers. Yet, Paul says that they were worshipping in ignorance (vs. 23). Is it possible today to be religious, to worship frequently, yet not really know the true God?

How does Paul's explanation of the true God challenge your own assumptions about who God really is?

Focus on verse 27. God has made it possible for you to "find God" if you seek after Him. God is not far from you in some distant galaxy. You can feel close to God every day. That is God's plan—to be in close, daily relationship with you.

Day 2
Opening Your Eyes to God's Presence

Read <u>2 Kings 6:8-17</u> several times and study this passage. God's presence was all around Elisha and his servant, yet the servant could not see God. The servant's eyes needed to be opened to see the spiritual realities all around him. We are the same way. To illustrate this point, we now know that microorganisms surround us. Yet, before humans invented the microscope and could observe them, we were unaware of their presence. Yet our ignorance did not make bacteria any less real. God's presence in our lives is not always immediately apparent. We must have our "eyes of faith" opened to be able to see God's presence all around us.

Read <u>Psalm 27:13.</u> This writer says that he almost lost his faith in "despair" because of his enemies (NASB). But he "believed" that he would see the goodness of the LORD in the land of the living. We must make the choice to see the good, and open the eyes of faith to see God in the events and situations of life.

Read <u>John 14:1-14</u> several times and study this passage. Philip, one of the twelve apostles, had personally lived with Jesus for three years. Yet, he asks Jesus to "show us the Father" (vs. 8). Philip wanted to experience God. Philip did not realize that he had been in the presence of God all along. Jesus says, "He who has seen me has seen the Father" (vs. 9). Often God is right in front of us, but we need to open our eyes and see Him.

Day 3
Experience God in Indirect Ways

Read <u>Exodus 33</u> several times and focus on this passage. Don't get bogged down in the details, but concentrate on the major themes. Focus on verse 11. What does this verse say about the relationship that Moses had with God?

Although Moses had a very intimate relationship with God (vs. 11), he desires to have a more *direct* encounter with God. God passes before Moses, allowing him to experience him *indirectly* (seeing his back-vs. 23). Man cannot experience God's presence *directly* in this life and live (vs. 20). It is clear that Moses had an intimate relationship with God, yet he only experienced God's presence *indirectly*.

Read <u>1 John 2:1-6</u> several times and focus on this passage. How does John say that we can be confident that we have an intimate relationship with God ("know Him")?

Day 4
Drawing Near to God

Read <u>James 4:8</u> and focus upon the first sentence. According to James, feeling close to God is dependent upon us first "drawing near to Him." You must first strive to get near to God by putting forth the effort to be close to Him, and then you will sense his presence coming closer to you.

Read <u>Jeremiah 29:13</u> and mediate upon this passage. Only the person who searches for God with "all their heart" will find him. You cannot search for God in a half-hearted way and expect to find Him.

Read <u>2 Chronicles 15:1-2</u>. God has promised to "let you find Him" if you seek Him.

Read <u>Psalm 42</u> several times and focus upon its message. To feel close to God, you must "thirst for Him" above everything else in life. You must "pour out your soul" to God and completely put your life into His hands.

Day 5
A Child/Parent Relationship with God

Read <u>Luke 11:1-13</u> several times and focus upon Jesus' message to you. Apparently as the disciples watched Jesus pray, they were impressed with the way he so freely and intimately talked with the Heavenly Father (vs. 1). As a result, the disciples wanted Jesus to teach them how to have such an intimate conversation with God, just as John had taught his disciples.

Jesus gives this prayer as a model to follow, not necessarily a formula to be recited. We should model our prayers to God after some of the major themes Jesus presents here. What are some of the main points Jesus is expressing in this prayer?

What does the tone of this prayer tell you about the relationship a disciple has with God? What does it tell you about the heart of a disciple?

In Jesus' teaching about prayer, why did the man grant the request of his neighbor at midnight (see verse 8)? What does this tell you about the way you should pray to God?

One of the main points of Jesus' teaching on prayer is that we are to have a relationship with God like a child with his/her father. Fathers do not grant all of the requests of their children (verses 11-13 qualify what Jesus means in verses 9-10). However, fathers are willing to grant anything to their children that will not be harmful to them. Fathers sometimes deny requests of their children because in their wisdom they know that such a request, if granted, will ultimately bring harm to them. For the same reason, sometimes God wisely denies our requests. However, God promises to "give good gifts" to us that are in our ultimate best interest.

Day 6
A Friend-Relationship with God

Read John 15:12-17 several times and focus upon Jesus' words to you. How does Jesus describe his great love for us (vs. 13)? How does it make you feel to know that not only did Jesus die for you, but he calls you his "friend?" What is the difference between a slave and a friend? Slaves blindly follow the commands of their taskmasters. Friends gladly do things for one another because of the love they share for each other.

How does it make you feel to know that the Creator of the Universe wants to be in a friendship with you?

How can we be confident that we have a strong friendship with God? (see verse 14).

Day 7
A Conversational Relationship with God

Read Hebrews 4:14-16 and reflect on the meaning of Jesus being our "high priest." During the time of Moses, God's presence descended upon a Mountain called Sinai in the form of smoke, fire, lightning, and thunder (cf. Exodus 19:18ff). The people of Israel were not allowed to come near the mountain or else they would die (cf. Exodus 19:12). Later, God's presence was in the "Most Holy Place" of the tabernacle (and later the Temple) (cf. Exodus 40:34-38). The people were separated from God by a veil that separated the "Most Holy Place" from the "Holy Place" and another curtain that divided the "Holy Place" from the courtyard. The people could not directly approach God; they had to have a priest who would mediate for them. The "high priest" would enter the "Most Holy Place" and approach God on behalf of the people. But the people themselves could not come close to God.

The writer of Hebrews in the New Testament explains that Jesus is the "great high priest" who did not simply go through the curtain of the tabernacle, rather, he "passed through the heavens" (Hebrews 4:14). Jesus can sympathize with our struggles as human beings because he faced all the same temptations. Yet, since Jesus was without personal sin, he went directly to the throne of Heaven. Followers of Jesus can "draw near with confidence to the throne of grace" (vs. 16).

How does it make you feel to know that you can have confidence to "draw near" to God in intimate conversation and friendship without fear or uncertainly?

Read Hebrews 10:19-22 several times and focus on the assurance we can have to draw near to God. New Christians often feel timid about being open, honest, and vulnerable before God in prayer. We often think, "God is too busy to be bothered with my problems." Or we may think we don't know the right "lofty-prayer-language" to use. Prayer is about friendship with God. On our own, we have no right to approach God in such a casual, conversational tone. However, we can do just that because of the "blood of Jesus" (vs. 19). We can have "full assurance of faith" because we have been sprinkled with Jesus' blood (vs. 22). We can "draw near" to God.

In a friendship, you cannot be close to someone if you don't spend time with them. You will never be intimate with your spouse, unless you spend lots of quality time with him or her. Likewise, the only way to "feel close to God" is to spend lots of time with him in the conversation of friendship—what the Bible calls prayer. Open yourself up to God. He wants to know your desires, doubts, and frustrations, your feelings of joy, sorrow, and anger. The best of friendships are built upon complete openness and honesty. Open yourself up to God. He wants to be your best friend.

Week 2
The Family of God

This week you will be studying the community of disciples called the family of God, or the church. God's family is described in terms of being the "body of Christ" of which every member is a valuable and needed part. This week you will be challenged to consider how God needs you as a functioning member of his heavenly family.

Day 1
The Structure of God's Family

Read <u>Ephesians 3:14-19</u> and consider the world-wide spiritual family of which you are now a part.

Read <u>Romans 8:12-17.</u> If you are being led by the Spirit of God, then you are living as one of God's children. God is not a Father to be feared, nor is being one of his children like slavery. We have been "adopted" into God's family, and we can cry out to God calling him "Abba" (similar to the English, "daddy"). Being fellow-heirs with Christ, we are siblings with Jesus.

Read <u>1 Corinthians 12:12-31</u> several times and focus on the structure of God's family—the "body of Christ."

Paul demonstrates in this passage that every member of the body of Christ is vitally important. Often, it is the least noticed (weaker members) that are the most crucial to the working of the body. Yet, the most noticed members, while very beneficial, are not the most needful. Even if you lost your eyesight, for example, your physical body could still live and function. However, if your lungs quit working you would cease to live. We rarely think about our lungs (except when something is wrong), yet they are crucial.

What abilities or talents has God given you that he expects you to use in his family?

Day 2
Preference for God's Family

Read <u>Romans 12:1-13</u> several times and focus on the message of these verses. Disciples must be humble toward one another. We are all equally in need of God's grace because of our personal sinfulness. No disciple of Christ is greater than the other. We are all saved by God's grace, not by our own works of righteousness. All of us have different talents and abilities given to us by God. We are all individually needed to make the "body of Christ" function. As disciples, we must prefer one another and work hard to "outdo one another is showing honor" for each other (vs. 10, ESV).

Read <u>Galatians 6:10</u> and consider the preference we are to show to God's household. Christians must go about doing good for all people, but our first obligation is to fellow believers. It is natural to feel close to our physical families. What will it take for you to feel even closer to your spiritual family?

Day 3
How to Treat One Another
in God's Family

Read 1 Peter 1:22-25 and focus upon the brotherly love we are to have for one another in God's family.

Read John 13:31-35. How will people in the world be able to identify a group of people as being truly disciples of Jesus?

Is it possible to be doctrinally right on many issues, yet not show love for your fellow disciples? Does doctrinal correctness, alone, make you a true disciple?

Read Colossians 3:12-15 several times and really focus on the way you are to treat fellow disciples in God's family. In these verses, what does Paul say you should do if you have a complaint against another disciple? What is the one thing that will bind together the family of God in perfect harmony (see verse 14)? The word translated "love" in the previous verse is the Greek word "*agape.*" This word describes an act of sacrificial service. This type of love is an action you take, not necessarily an emotion you "feel." Putting on "love" (*agape*) toward others is something you choose to do, even if you don't feel like it.

Read Ephesians 4:1-6 and concentrate on what we must do in order to maintain unity as the "one body" of Christ. What does it mean to "bear with one another in love" (vs. 2, ESV)?

Day 4
Learning to Lean Upon Each Other

Read <u>James 5:16</u>. Why do you think it is important for disciples to confess their sins to one another?

Read <u>Acts 19:11-20.</u> Believers specifically confessed their sinful practices before other believers and then visibly burned their books of sorcery. Confessing your sins before fellow believers provides great spiritual strength. Disciples must help hold one another accountable in their battles against sin.

Read <u>Hebrews 10:19-25</u> several times, and focus on the message. What bad habit had some of these disciples developed?

Why is it so important to consistently meet with other disciples in regular gatherings? What should disciples be doing for one another when they meet together? (see vs. 24 and 25).

There is an old story about two men who were sitting together watching a fire in the fireplace, and one asked the other the importance of attending church. The older Christian slowly took the tongs and pulled a red hot coal from the fire and laid it alone at one side. They sat and watched the coal grow darker and darker until the coal was cold and black. The younger Christian said, "I understand."

Day 5
Loyalty to One Another

Read 1 John 3:13-15 several times and consider how serious it is to have hatred in your heart for a fellow disciple.

The main assignment for today is to read 1 John 4:7-21 numerous times and deeply meditate on this important instruction. Summarize the message of this text in your own words below:

Day 6
Watching Out For One Another

Read Galatians 6:1-2 several times and focus on the message. According to this verse, what responsibility do you have toward fellow believers? We must be careful when pointing out the weaknesses of other disciples. We all have our own struggles and temptations. We must have a humble attitude toward one another, realizing that we are all helping each other get to heaven. We must learn to "bear one another's burdens."

Read James 5:19-20 several times and focus on the passage. What obligation do we have toward one another if we wander from the truth?

Read Jude 1:20-23 and meditate on the message. Depending upon the situation, we must use wisdom in dealing with each other according to the need of the moment. At times we need to be gentle in correcting one another and at other times we must "snatch" one another from the flames of fire.

Day 7
What is "Fellowship" in the Family of God?

Read Acts 2:42 and consider the things to which the earliest disciples were continually devoted. It is important to see that our early brothers and sisters were just as concerned about devoting themselves to "fellowship" as they were devoting themselves to the apostles' teaching, the Lord's Supper or to prayer. The word translated "fellowship" here is the Greek word *koinonia* which literally means: "close association involving mutual interests and sharing; association; communion; fellowship, close relationship; community, communion, or intimacy." The early disciples devoted themselves to working hard to develop, nurture, and maintain deep, authentic relationships with one another. They had a deep sense of community with one another.

Read 1 John 1:1-4 several times and consider the "fellowship" that we are to have with one another and with God. The same word (*koinonia*) is used here in this passage. Our community and intimacy is to be with God the Father, His Son Jesus Christ, and with each other.

What are you doing to help develop deep, authentic relationships with other disciples in the local church of which you are a part?

Week 3
Right Relationships

This week you will be studying God's instructions on how to have right relationships with others in this life. Jesus provides relationship principles that are vastly different than our normal inclinations of human interaction. The instructions God gives on healthy relationships may challenge the way that you normally are accustomed to functioning in relationships with others.

Day 1
The Primary Relationship

Read <u>Matthew 12:46-50</u> several times and mediate upon the way Jesus viewed his family relationships. Do you think Jesus was being unloving toward his mother and brothers? What does Jesus' example here teach you about the priority you put upon your relationships with physical family compared with your spiritual family?

Have your relationships with family and friends changed since you became a disciple of Jesus? If so, how?

Read <u>Matthew 10:32-39</u> several times and consider the seriousness of Jesus' teaching. In what ways might being a genuine disciple of Jesus make you an "enemy" with members of your own family? There have been many people who were faced with the ultimatum by family members, "It is either me or this Christ-thing." Have you been faced with this decision? If you were, how would you handle it?

Read <u>1 Corinthians 7:12-15</u>. In these verses, the Bible gives instruction to a new convert who is faced with a "me or Christ"

ultimatum by their spouse. Paul says that your loyalty to Christ is more important than your loyalty to your spouse (vs. 15). Are you willing to put your devotion to Christ above your spouse?

Read Matthew 19:29. Does this saying of Jesus give you any encouragement on this topic? Do you think, ultimately, it would be worth it to choose Christ over your own physical family?

Day 2
Your New Family Comes First

Read James 4:4 several times and consider what the Scripture is saying to you. How does God feel if you try and be friends with him while also embracing the values and desires of the world?

Read John 15:18-25. Why does the world "hate" disciples of Jesus Christ?

Read Colossians 4:5-6. How should disciples of Jesus view associations with people in the world who are not followers of Christ?

Read 2 Corinthians 6:14-18. Why might it be spiritually dangerous for disciples to have close partnerships with unbelievers?

Read 1 Corinthians 9:1-5. Paul was not married; however in these verses he demonstrates that he has the freedom to marry if he chose to do so. He says he has the right to choose a "believing wife" (vs. 5). Why would Paul choose to limit himself to choosing a Christian spouse?

Day 3
Dealing with an Unbelieving Spouse

Read 1 Peter 3:1-7 several times and focus upon Peter's instructions to disciples with unbelieving spouses. In the first-century when the message of Jesus was first circulating, often women were the first to respond to the gospel message (cf. Acts 16:13-15). Knowing that they had an obligation to be submissive to their unbelieving husbands, these women were faced with a challenging situation. In these verses, Peter addresses this difficulty.

Peter tells wives to continue to be submissive to their husbands. These women should not nag their husbands about their lack of faith. Rather, they should let their Christ-like behavior and actions speak for themselves. Without saying a word, unbelieving husbands can be won to Christ by watching the pure and respectful behavior of their wives.

Genuine faith lived out in the life of a person is often a much stronger persuading force than a verbal lecture. Let your changed way of life speak for itself. If you are a believing husband with an unbelieving wife, this approach still applies.

Day 4
God's Plan for Marriage

Read Matthew 19:1-12 several times and focus upon this teaching of Christ. What does Jesus say was God's original intention for marriage? Why, then, does Jesus say that Moses permitted divorce?

Jesus restores God's original purpose for marriage—one man and one woman for life.

What does Jesus say happens if you divorce your spouse and marry another person? **Read Matthew 5:31-32.** What other detail does Jesus add to this topic?

What *exception* does Jesus give to this general principle?

Read Malachi 2:14-16. Christians are called by God to keep the covenants that they make. Why do you think God takes covenant faithfulness so seriously?

Read 1 Corinthians 7:10-16. How much of a priority should Christians place upon nourishing and maintaining their marriages?

Day 5
Divine Instruction for Conflict Resolution

Read <u>Matthew 5:21-26</u> several times, and focus upon Jesus' teaching about interpersonal relationships. How important does Jesus indicate that it is to resolve conflicts with other disciples? Is there a time when *not going to church* is actually the right thing to do?

Carefully read <u>Matthew 18:15-17,</u> and outline the steps that Jesus says we are to take in resolving conflict with fellow believers.

STEP#1: _____

STEP #2: _____

STEP #3: _____

What is your natural tendency when you are having interpersonal conflicts with others? How do you normally deal with it?

Often we tend to ignore the problem (and it usually only gets worse, not better), or we talk to other people about the problem (sometimes in the form of gossip), or we indirectly hint at the problem with the person and hope that they get the point.

Jesus says that we have an obligation to go directly to the person with whom we are having conflict and address the issue head on in a private setting. Confronting someone who has sinned against us is never easy, but it is easier than the eroding relationship that will result if action is not taken.

Day 6
Learning the Spirit of Forgiveness

Read Matthew 18:21-35 several times and make personal application from Jesus' teaching. Jewish Rabbis taught that you should forgive someone three times. Peter understood that Jesus calls his followers to higher conduct than the Jewish teachers. Peter doubles the figure and adds an extra one for good measure. Should I forgive someone seven times? Jesus makes the point that we should not keep track of how many times we forgive someone. Forgiveness is a lifestyle choice; it is not a single event based upon your feelings toward someone.

In Jesus' parable, the man who owed billions of dollars was forgiven the debt when he could not pay. Yet the same man found someone who owed him a few dollars and demanded payment. In the story the king says, *"Should not you have had mercy on your fellow servant, as I had mercy on you?"* Jesus says that God demands that I "forgive my brother from the heart" when he offends me if I expect God's forgiveness toward me.

Read Matthew 6:14-15 and let these verses sink into your heart. How important is it that you have a forgiving spirit toward other people? Forgiveness is not as much about the other person as it is about you.

By forgiving, you free your spirit from the chains of bitterness that tie you to the one who hurt you. You can choose to forgive. That does not mean that you are "letting them off the hook," as if their actions don't have consequences. Jesus provided forgiveness of our sins by absorbing our debts for us. We are called to forgive, and it requires painfully absorbing the debt of those who wrong us. While a painful process, forgiveness ultimately frees your own spirit.

Consider: What if forgiveness wasn't dependent upon the degree to which someone has wronged you but the degree to which God has forgiven you?

Who do you need to forgive this week?

Day 7
Establishing Healthy Boundaries

Read <u>Romans 12:9-21</u> several times and focus on what these verses teach about how disciples react to other people. It is never right for you to seek revenge or retaliate against someone who hurts you. Don't be overcome with wicked behavior by returning evil-for-evil. Don't lower yourself to that same level. Instead, return good for evil.

Christians must have forgiving spirits. However, sometimes it is not possible to live in peaceful interaction with others. You must do everything you can to live peaceably with others. At times this may mean establishing healthy boundaries. Establishing boundaries does not mean that you build walls around your heart, isolating yourself from people. Jesus came to destroy the walls that divide people (see Ephesians 2:14).

What is the difference between building walls in your relationships and establishing healthy boundaries?

Read <u>Matthew 5:37</u> and <u>James 5:12</u> and consider what it means to "let your 'no,' be 'no'." We must be courageous enough to say "no" and mean it. It is not loving or Christian to let people misuse you or walk over you. Christians must be "meek" (humble, gentle), but that does not mean that we are to be "weak." Jesus withdrew and kept some people at a distance when they were tempting him to lose his spiritual focus (see Matthew 16:23; Luke 8:19-21; John 2:4; John 6:15).

Is there someone in your life that is preventing you from having a spiritual focus? A friend? A family member? How do you need to establish healthy boundaries with this person?

Week 4
Worship

This week you will be studying the meaning of true worship. There are lots of different styles of worship taking place today, and everyone seems to have an opinion as to what makes for good worship. In this lesson you will focus on what God asks from you *personally* for worship.

Day 1
What is Worship?

Read <u>Matthew 4:1-11</u> several times and especially focus on Jesus' response to being tempted to worship someone other than God. The English word "worship" means "showing reverence for a deity with religious rites; intense love or admiration." God wants us to worship Him. What does this mean? He wants us to show reverence (respect) for Him, yes. But he also wants us to have intense love for Him.

Read <u>Exodus 4:31.</u> There are several words in the Bible that are translated "worship." One of the most notable (in the New Testament) is the Greek word "*proskuneo*" which literally means to "kiss the hand to." This word presents the picture of falling upon your knees with your forehead to the ground as an act of extreme reverence. In worship, we bow our spirits before God.

Read <u>Luke 18:9-14</u>. What was the difference between the Pharisee's worship and the tax collector's worship?

Day 2
Worship in Spirit and Truth

Read John 4:19-24 and focus on the type of worshippers that God desires. Jesus makes clear that the physical location of worship is not important. Rather, it is the location of your heart that is vital. He says that true worshippers will be recognized by the way they worship. There are two requirements for "true worship." It must be in "spirit and truth." To worship in truth means to reverence God in a true and genuine way. To worship "in spirit" refers to your inner being, the very place where the Holy Spirit indwells the believer. Worship is where our human spirits deeply connect with God's Spirit.

How might your worship become imbalanced?

What would worship *in truth* but *not spirit* look like?

What would worship *in spirit* but *not truth* look like?

Day 3
Acceptable Worship

Read Hebrews 12:28-29 and consider the importance of worshipping God in an "acceptable" way. God wants us to worship him, but he defines the type of worship he wants. If there is a type of worship God finds acceptable, that implies that some attempts at worship he would find unacceptable (cf. Lev. 10:1-3). God wants us to treat him with holiness, and approach him with respect. Acceptable worship is done with reverence and awe. Worship to God must never be flippant but offered with great awareness of God's majesty and holiness.

God wants us to approach him and draw near to him in worship, while also being respectful of his glory and majesty.

How might being *too fearful* of God inhibit your worship?

How might not having *sufficient fear* be harmful to worship?

Day 4
Joyful Worship

Read <u>Psalm 33:1-9</u> and meditate on the attitude God wants you to have when you worship him. God desires that we come before him with joyful singing (vs. 1). He does not ask for lifeless, somber chants. God wants jubilant praise! More than just a power to be feared, God is the center of true joy and delight and is to be enjoyed and celebrated.

He wants us to sing a "new song" to him (vs. 3a). Repetitive and familiar songs can become stale to the heart. Continually bringing fresh expressions of praise to God keeps the heart stirred and affectionate toward him.

He wants us to bring our best worship to him in skillful ways (vs. 3b). We should strive to make our praise beautiful.

God welcomes exuberant praise (vs. 3c). He desires that we "shout for joy" when we worship him. Instead of coming before God on tiptoes and whispers, he wants us to come with a shout. Our God welcomes energetic and celebratory praise.

Why do you think this passage specifically tells us to sing a "new song" to God? What might cold and lifeless worship do to a person's relationship with God?

Day 5
Participation, Not Performance

Read Matthew 6:1-18 several times and consider the difference between participatory worship and performance worship. Jesus tells us to "beware of practicing our righteousness before other people in order to be seen by them" (vs. 1). How do you think God feels about performance worship?

What worship activities might tend to be performance-oriented and actually hinder worship participation?

Read Ephesians 5:15-20 and notice the shared nature of worshipping God from the Spirit. God desires that we sing and make music from our hearts to him. Our praise to God comes in the form of psalms, hymns and songs from the Spirit. Being filled with the Spirit, we are to speak "to one another" in our praise to God. Worship is an activity in which God wants us each to individually participate, not a performance we spectate.

How important do you think it is for you to personally participate in worship with other Christians?

What things might hinder you from worshipping God? How might you overcome these roadblocks?

Day 6
Sacrifice of Praise

Read Hebrews 13:15 and think about how worship is described to us. Our worship is to be "through" Jesus. We are to offer *continual* praise to God. The worship we offer to God through Christ is better than any sacrifice of the Old Covenant. Our worship is a sweet aroma to God. Through our worship we acknowledge the name of God with our devotion to him evidenced with a song pouring from our lips.

In what sense might worship be considered a "sacrifice" offered to God?

How might worship require a sacrifice from you?

Read Romans 12:1-2 and consider the type of sacrifice God wants from you. More than just an isolated event, worship should be a lifestyle that characterizes the disciple. God is pleased when we offer our bodies to him as a living sacrifice. More than simply engaging in obligatory rituals, God wants us to surrender our lives to him.

How might you present your body as a living sacrifice in everyday life?

What does this passage add to your understanding of true worship?

Day 7
God's Presence in Our Worship

Read 1 Corinthians 14:24-25 and consider how God is present with you when you worship with other believers. When unbelievers visited the worship gatherings of early Christians, they were overwhelmed at what they witnessed. Seeing the power and presence of God among the worshippers, these guests would fall on their faces and proclaim, *"God* *is really among you!"* Worship gatherings should a be a place where we encounter the presence of God and are overwhelmed by his glorious majesty.

In what ways might we welcome God's presence to be among us in our worship?

How might we actually hinder the presence of God in our gatherings?

Read Psalm 22:3 and delight in the truth that God dwells in the praises of his people. When we come together with other believers and join in praise to God, God's comes to dwell within the praise itself. If you are going through a difficult time of life, start praising God, and you have his promise that he will come to dwell within your praise.

When you are really struggling in life, do you tend to complain to God or praise him? In what ways might this verse challenge your tendency?

Read Hebrews 2:9-13 and come to realize that Jesus joins us in the congregation when we worship. Jesus considers his followers to be his very own brothers and sisters. We are part of the same family. Not only does he claim us as his siblings, but he joins us when we sing praise to God in our assemblies.

How might realizing that Jesus is sitting beside you in worship, joining the song, affect the way you worship?

Week 5
Submission

This week you will be studying the concept of Biblical submission. Conventional wisdom in our culture is opposed to the idea of submission. Jesus, however, perfectly models the concept of submission and commands his followers to also be submissive.

Day 1
What is Biblical Submission?

Read <u>1 Peter 1:2, 14.</u> What kind of children does God desire? Being obedient means that we are willing to voluntarily submit to someone else.

Read <u>Ephesians 2:1-2.</u> God is opposed to people that have what kind of spirit?

Read <u>Hebrews 5:7-9.</u> What did Jesus learn while he was upon the earth in human flesh? How did he learn this? If we follow Jesus, what does God want us to learn? How do we learn this?

The old self does not like to be told what to do. Our sinful desires do not want to obey. Satan is the Father of rebellion. Likewise, those who follow earthly ways will also despise all authority (see 2 Peter 2:10). Following Christ, however, is about learning to obey the commands of God. When we become disciples of Jesus, we are volunteering to "deny ourselves" and our own ways and submit to what God says is best for our lives.

Day 2
Submit to One Another

Read <u>Ephesians 5:15-21</u> and focus especially on verse 21. Paul says that we are to *"submit to one another out of reverence for Christ."* The reason that disciples are willing to be submissive to other people is because of their respect for Jesus Christ. Conflicts, wars, arguments, disagreements, and feuds between people can usually be traced back to selfishness, pride, jealousy and envy.

Read <u>Philippians 2:1-8</u> several times and reflect upon how Jesus modeled submission for his followers. We are to be humble toward one another and consider other people as being more significant than ourselves. If anyone ever had a right to be boastful and arrogant, it was the Son of God. Yet, Jesus humbled himself and was willing to serve his fellow man. If Jesus can practice submission, then certainly so can his followers.

Day 3
Submit to God

Read <u>James 4:1-7</u> and especially focus upon verses 6-7. God is opposed to proud, arrogant people. When we think that we are self-sufficient and don't need others, then God cannot work in our lives.

The grace of God can work only in the life of the person who has humbled himself/herself. It is only when you acknowledge your inadequacy and your dependence upon God that his grace and power can work in your life. You must make a concerted, conscious effort to voluntarily submit your life to God's control. As one bumper sticker reads, *"If God is your co-pilot, swap seats!"*

Read <u>Matthew 25:31-46</u> and consider the difference between sheep and goats. Goats do what they want. They are rebellious creatures that follow their own path. Sheep, on the other hand, naturally and voluntarily follow their shepherd. People that follow their own way will find their end in destruction. Those who submit to God will find eternal life.

Day 4
Submit to Your Spiritual Leaders

Read <u>1 Peter 5:1-5</u> several times and focus on why younger people are commanded to submit to their elders. Who do you think has more of a tendency to rebel against authority figures: older people or younger people? Why? Why are younger people inclined to reject the council and advice of older, experienced people?

In the church, God has commanded that every local congregation be led by a group of qualified elders (see 1 Timothy 3:1-7; Titus 1:5-9; Acts 14:23). These elders (or shepherds) are to spiritually guide, correct, and council people in the church. Read <u>1 Thessalonians 5:12-14.</u>

Read <u>Hebrews 13:17.</u> Why does scripture say that you are to obey and submit to the spiritual leaders that are over you in the local church?

Read <u>Hebrews 10:19-27</u>. How serious is it that we not neglect the times that the local church meets together? What is the purpose of the church gathering together regularly? What type of attitude should we have toward the spiritual guidance and equipping that church leaders provide?

Day 5
Wives Submit to Their Husbands

Read <u>1 Peter 3:1-7</u> several times and focus on Scripture's instructions to husbands and wives. What effect can a woman's submissive demeanor have upon an unbelieving husband? Husbands are to live with their wives in an understanding way. Men must understand that women have a more delicate physical body and are generally more emotional than men. Husbands must protect their wives from physical and emotional harm. Men who lovingly protect and love their wives will earn respect, and most wives will gladly submit to their leadership.

Read <u>Colossians 3:18-19</u>. Scripture says here that it is "fitting in the Lord" for wives to voluntarily submit to their husbands. Husbands are commanded to love their wives (verse 19) and "not be harsh with them." What connection might gentleness have with submission?

Read <u>Ephesians 5:22-30</u> several times, and consider the roles of husbands and wives toward one another. Scripture teaches that husbands are to be the spiritual leaders of the home. Wives are to submit to the leadership of their husbands "as to the Lord" (verse 22). This does not mean that a husband is "the boss of his wife" or is justified in being domineering in the home. What kind of sacrificial love did Jesus model for husbands (verse 25)?

Day 6
Submission to Governing Authorities

Read <u>1 Peter 2:13-17</u> several times and consider the responsibility Christians have to be obedient to political and governing authorities. The first readers of this letter lived under a harsh Roman

Emperor that would sporadically persecute Christians. Yet, Peter instructs them to "honor the emperor." Christians should live humble, peaceable lives in society that demonstrate that we are not a rebellious group. How might your passion for politics actually ruin your Christian witness in the world?

Read Romans 13:1-7. If we resist governing authorities, these verses say we are resisting God, who appointed these authorities. God appoints political leadership in nations to keep peace and order. Those who obey the law have no reason to fear. Christians are to be law abiding citizens and submit to the governing authorities. In what ways do you find it most difficult to submit to the government?

Read Mark 12:13-17. Jesus teaches his disciples that we must give governing authorities our submission (paying taxes, obeying set laws, etc.), but we must also give God our submission. These are two separate areas of submission. However, if submission to governing authorities means that we must disobey God, then it is "better to obey God than man" (Acts 5:29). When might civil disobedience be a necessary component to the Christian's life?

Day 7
Things To Which You Should Not Submit

Read Colossians 2:20-23 several times and determine what Paul is warning against. These religious teachers were trying to impose self-made religious regulations upon people. Such is common today as well. Religious teachers and leaders are often guilty of imposing man-made rules upon other people in the name of religion. Such is often an attempt to control people. When have you seen this?

Disciples of Jesus must submit to God and his commands as taught in the Scriptures. However, you must be aware that there are people who will try and mislead you and take advantage of your loyalty to Christ. You are under no obligation to submit to the self-made religious rules that people promote and teach. Be a careful student of God's word, and exercise your spiritual senses to discern the difference between good and evil and the difference between God's commands and the religious opinions and teachings of men.

Week 6
Sharing Jesus with Others

This week you will be studying about sharing your new-found faith with other people. Christianity is a taught religion. You have been saved by God's grace because someone taught you. It is now your responsibility and privilege to share the message of how to experience a relationship with God.

Day 1
An Exciting, Contagious Faith

Read Jeremiah 20:9. What does this prophet mean when he says that the message of God was like a "fire in his bones" that he could not hold inside?

Read Romans 1:16-17. We must not be ashamed to share our faith with other people. You can have confidence in sharing this message with others because your effectiveness is not dependent upon your own ability or speech. The power of the gospel for salvation is found in the "power of God."

Read Isaiah 6:1-8 and notice that God needs people that he can send. What attitude does Isaiah have toward God's call for volunteers? What is your attitude?

Read 2 Corinthians 5 slowly and mediate upon the "ministry of reconciliation" that God has given to you. To reconcile means to bring separated people back together. As a disciple, you have been given the ministry of helping bring other people back to God. Who do you want to focus your efforts upon to bring them into a deeper relationship with God?

Day 2
Having Spiritual Confidence

Read 1 John 5:13-15 and think about the confidence you can have in your salvation. In these verses, John makes clear his purpose for writing this letter: you can be certain about your salvation. God does not want you to live doubting that you are saved. Why would having doubts about your personal salvation make it hard to share your faith with others?

Read 1 John 1 several times and notice when you have the promise of the continual cleansing of Jesus' blood. The promise of continual forgiveness is given to those who are "walking in the light" in continual fellowship with God.

Your salvation does not depend upon your own works of righteousness or by perfectly keeping all God's commands. No one will always "do their best." Christians must recognize that they are sinners (see 1 John 1:8), and all of our righteous deeds are like filthy rags in God's sight (Isaiah 64:6). Your salvation is dependent upon what Christ did for you. You can be absolutely confident that you are continually saved as long as you remain connected in your relationship to Christ (see John 15:1-11).

If you are a disciple of Jesus, you have eternal life and will never misplace it, as long as you walk daily with Jesus. In your walk there will be times that you stumble (sin) and fall. But you are still saved, and Christ will pick you up, as long as you continue walking with Him.

Read John 10:27-29, and notice the promise Jesus gives that you can be confident in your salvation. It is possible to forfeit your salvation and turn your back on God in unbelief (Hebrews 3:12). But if your heart longs for Jesus, then nobody and nothing can *forcibly* remove you from his hand. No one can separate you from Jesus' love (Romans 8:37-39). There is nothing more peaceful and encouraging than being confident in your salvation. Anyone that submits their lives to Jesus can have this kind of confidence. Everyone is looking for spiritual peace, and you can show them how to receive it! But you will only be able teach others God's way when you personally have the joy and confidence of your own salvation (Psalm 51:12-13).

Day 3
Sharing What Jesus Has Done for You

Read John 9:1-25 slowly and consider the example of the blind man that was healed. This man was not interested in entering into a theological debate with the Pharisees. He was not interested in participating in a religious argument. Neither was he prepared to answer complex questions about how he was healed. But his man's statement is profound, *"One thing I do know, that though I was blind, now I see"* (vs. 25). He simply shared with other people what Jesus had personally done for him.

The most effective evangelism is often the simple approach of sharing your personal spiritual journey with someone else. Theology often confuses people. Religious arguments frequently alienate folks. But genuine life-testimony resonates. It is hard to argue against a completely transformed life.

Spend some time thinking about your personal spiritual story. Think about what Jesus has done in your life personally. How has your life been changed by becoming a disciple? How has your life been made better? Pray that God will give you opportunity soon to share your story with someone. When the opportunity comes, courageously walk through the door.

Day 4
Making a Defense of Your Hope

Read 1 Peter 3:13-17 several times focusing upon the message of this passage (concentrate on verses 15 and 16). Consider the following statements in these verses. What do each of these phrases say to you about sharing your faith with others?

"In your hearts honor Christ the Lord as holy"

_____

"always be prepared to make a defense to anyone who asks you for the reason for the hope that is in you"

_____

"do it with gentleness and respect"

_____

"having a good conscience"

_____

Write down the names of some of your friends or family who are not Christians. Speaking their specific names, pray that God will help you to share your faith with them. Focus on using principles learned above in your approach to reach them for Christ.

_____

_____

_____

Day 5
Walk in Wisdom with Seasoned Speech

Read <u>Colossians 4:5-6</u> several times and mediate on the way you are to behave around unbelievers. There are wise and unwise ways to conduct yourself as a disciple around unbelievers. You must learn to "pick your battles," and make the most of the opportunities that are presented you to share your faith.

Forcing spiritual conversations at unnatural times often proves to be counter-productive. You must look for moments when people are receptive to spiritual discussion. Try and find opportunities to naturally bridge your normal conversation into spiritual discussions. "Make the most of the time" that you have with unbelievers.

Don't be forceful, harsh, or combative in your conversation with outsiders. If you win a religious argument but lose the soul of the person with whom you are talking, you lost the battle for the Lord. Let your language be filled with graciousness. Be understanding and patient with them—give them the benefit of the doubt. Try and get in their shoes and look at life from their unique perspective.

The wonderful message of Jesus can become bitter and disgusting to the unbeliever who hears the message in a harsh and bitter tone. The speech we choose must be carefully "seasoned as with salt" to make it as palatable as possible. We must never compromise the message of God's truth, but we must speak it in a spirit of genuine concern and love (Ephesians 4:15).

You cannot approach all people the same way. Ask God for wisdom and direction to help you know how you should "answer each person." Every person is different, and each individual deserves a tailor-made approach to hearing the gospel in a way that fits their situation and personality.

Day 6
Don't Be Quarrelsome
But Teach with Gentleness

Read 2 Timothy 2:22-26 several times and consider the attitude you are to have as the Lord's bondservant. Many have turned away from God because an overenthusiastic disciple of Jesus allowed a spiritual conversation to turn into a spiritual argument. Scripture tells us here that we must *"have nothing to do with foolish, ignorant controversies,"* and we should avoid quarrels.

As the Lord's servant, you must "be kind to everyone" even those who are not kind to you. When sharing your faith, some people will quickly become combative. Do not allow yourself to be lowered to this level. The bondservant of the Lord must always be kind and gentle. There is a time to correct the religious error that people believe. But when we try to correct people, we must do so in gentleness (verse 25). We must understand that people who hold false doctrines have been ensnared by the devil. Pray that God will work in this person's life, using you as an instrument, that they might repent from their incorrect beliefs and escape the trap of the devil. How have you seen patience and gentleness diffuse tense conversations?

Day 7
Jesus' Final Command & Promise

Read <u>Matthew 28:18-20</u> several times and meditate upon Jesus' final command. It is important to take note of someone's final words. Jesus' final command to his followers before his ascension back to heaven was that we must be busy making other disciples.

Our job is to train people to be followers of Christ. Making disciples of Jesus involves two things: (1) baptizing them in the name of the Father, Son and Holy Spirit (2) and teaching them to observe all that Jesus commanded.

If you have never talked to someone else about Jesus, you may be nervous about it. You may feel like you are not equipped, knowledgeable enough, or strong enough to share your faith. Ironically, you *should not* trust in yourself when sharing your faith! By your own power, you will never convert anyone. The power of salvation is found only in "the power of God" (Romans 1:16).

Pray to God and ask him to use you and give you wisdom about what to say and how to say it. Jesus gives a great promise with his command that we make disciples: "*And behold, I am with you always.*" When you are sharing your faith with someone else, you can be confident that Jesus is really right there with you. Lean upon him and trust that his presence and his word will do the converting.

Read <u>1 Corinthians 3:5-6</u>. We are servants that God uses to do his work. We "plant" and "water," but it is God who will give the increase. How does trusting God for the "results" relieve the pressure of sharing your faith?

Appendix

Disciple-Maker's Guide

Sharing My Faith: Where Do I Start?

Three Stories

There is power in a well-told story. The Bible records God's interaction with the world, the greatest story ever told. Of all the types of writing in the Bible, 43% is narrative (stories). The Bible presents a unified story that all leads to Jesus.[72] The gospel is not primarily what we do for God, but instead is the story of what God has done for us. It is not foremost commands to be obeyed, but instead it is "good news" to be proclaimed. The Gospel Story is God's greatest gift to the human race. It is a story you must hear. But in order for stories to be heard, they must be told. Followers of Jesus are on a mission to share the Gospel Story with the world. But what is the best way to do this? It is actually easier than you might think. If you're in a relationship with Jesus, you already have everything you need to share the Gospel Story with someone else. There are three steps.

First: Their Story

Talking to someone about spiritual things is a very personal and vulnerable thing. We must earn the right to be heard. So sharing the Gospel Story begins with the Golden Rule—"*do to others whatever you would like them to do to you*" (Matthew 7:12, NLT). Sharing your faith begins by building spiritual friendships. Friendships are built upon trust, safety, and active listening. The first stage of sharing your faith is working hard to create and cultivate a meaningful relationship of trust with another person. Before we have the right to speak truth into someone's life, we must first pay relational rent. Here are several practical tips for forming spiritual friendships: [73]

1. *Show yourself to be a safe person to talk to about spiritual things.* We are constantly trying to get a read on the motivations of others. If we react, get defensive or are quick to argue, we disqualify ourselves as a spiritual friend. You earn the right to be heard by serving, listening, caring, smiling and showing yourself to be a friendly, safe person.

2. *Use everyday vocabulary.* Using religious jargon can be confusing and even off-putting to non-Christians. Find ways to naturally explain your faith in conversational, everyday language.

3. *Instead of trying to "prove" what is true, help others "discover" what is true.* Many postmodern people today are very educated and want to enter a process of discovery. Instead of positioning yourself as a teacher, be a friend who gives space for others to come to conclusions for themselves.

4. *Don't be a religious debater; be a spiritual coach.* Avoid "win-lose" arguments. Give space for people to think and grow for themselves. Like a midwife facilitating a birth, instead of trying to convert someone to your ideas, enter into spiritual life with others.

5. *Instead of resolving every issue that arises, work to keep the conversation going.* There is a time and season for everything. Not every misunderstanding needs to be immediately addressed. Instead of telling others what to believe, respond with questions to keep your friend thinking. It is possible to accept a person and accept their beliefs and feelings as genuine without endorsing or agreeing with those beliefs. The objective is not to win arguments, but to win souls. Keep the conversation open.

6. *Move away from denominational competition, and work to move people closer to Jesus.* Instead of trying to convince people to join your group, work to help them to have a deeper relationship with Christ and be a better disciple of his. The mission is to make disciples of Jesus, not just church loyalists.

7. *Humbly demonstrate you are on equal footing.* We each are in need of God's grace and a deeper walk with Christ. Approach your friend from the perspective of genuinely trying to deepen your own relationship with Christ. Show that you are both sitting at the feet of Christ and his word.

8. *Use speech that is filled with grace and demonstrate gentleness.* We must be wise toward non-Christians with conversations filled with grace (Colossians 4:5-6). We must never be argumentative but always gentle (2 Timothy 2:24-26).

9. *Listen and take others seriously* (Proverbs 18:13). We should not expect others to take us seriously if we're not willing to take them seriously. It is important to understand what people are saying and clearly see their perspective. Such disarms and puts us in a position to empathize and respond redemptively.

10. *Avoid falsely presenting the other side* (Proverbs 21:28). Practicing the Golden Rule, we should never misrepresent someone's argument with a straw man. Such provokes distrust and hostility toward the one we are trying to reach.

11. *Resist assuming motives* (Proverbs 16:2; 20:5). We can only speculate about motives and should not try and demonize people. We should not be overly quick to judge motives, but discern deeper issues and avoid jumping to conclusions.

12. ***Find points of agreement to affirm*** (Proverbs 15:1). The goal is not to win the argument but win the person. To win a person, we must look for connecting points and find common ground.

13. ***Resist focusing on the periphery*** (Proverbs 13:10). We need to stay focused on the big picture, and resist the tendency to respond to every point with which we may disagree. Not every objection should be treated with the same priority. We must distinguish between the essentials and the periphery. Often challenges are not about essential doctrine but about doctrines inherited from theological traditions. Not every issue is critical. Keep the discussion open by not creating unnecessary boundaries.

14. ***Avoid being unnecessarily antagonistic*** (Proverbs 20:3). Avoid derogatory language, mocking, or making their view look silly. Such only alienates people. We should interact with godly wisdom and sensitivity, loving and praying for those who are pre-Christian.

Real humility opens doors for understanding. Your aim is to help folks be in sympathy with believers and help remove some doubts. To do this, we must treasure people the way God does. When you engage in defensive arguments, you lose your capacity to deal with people as precious, valuable souls.[74] You lose the heart of Christianity. You can be strong in your affirmations without becoming defensive. So, remain humble toward God and others.

Second: Your Story

One of the most compelling examples of faith-sharing in the gospels is found in Mark 5 where Jesus heals a demon-possessed man. Freed from his bondage, he begs to accompany Jesus. Yet, Jesus says something (vs. 19) very instructive:

"Go home to your own people and tell them how much the Lord has done for you, and how he has had mercy on you."

Here Jesus provides three principles of how to effectively share your faith with others.

1. **Go to your own people.** Sharing Jesus starts with going to your "own people." Who are "your people?" They are the people you have invested in relationally, with whom you are building trust and have influence.

2. **Share how much the Lord has done for you.** You don't have to be a religious expert. All you need to know is what the Lord has personally done for you, and be willing to share it openly.

3. **Share the power of grace.** Everyone has a story to tell of how they have been shown God's mercy and grace. Your story of experiencing grace means sharing how you have been set free from bondage in your life because of Christ.

As we live with Christ, there will be times when others will notice the contrast between our lives and the ways of the world. In those moments, we will be asked about the reason why we have hope (1 Peter 3:15). At that time, we must be prepared to share our story of faith. Giving a testimonial of the Lord's power in your life is something modeled three times by Paul in the book of Acts (Acts 9, 22, 26). He shared his attitude and actions prior to his conversion (Acts 26:1-11), the circumstances surrounding his conversion (Acts 26:12-18), and his attitudes and actions after his conversion (Acts 26:19-23). This provides a model for also crafting our own testimonial stories of hope.[75] Sharing our own stories make us interesting and relatable to others. It is hard to argue with the power of a changed life. As Chuck Swindoll has said, *"The skeptic may deny your doctrine or attack your church, but he cannot honestly ignore the fact that your life has been changed."*

As you prepare your own testimonial story of hope, there are three "acts" to every story:

1. ***Act 1: Before.*** Describe your attitudes, actions, feelings and relationships before you became a follower of Christ.

2. ***Act 2: During.*** Describe the time, place, circumstances, motivations and people surrounding your conversion. What realization finally motivated you to follow Jesus? How did the gospel of Jesus' death, burial and resurrection affect you?

3. ***Act 3: After.*** Describe the benefits you have experienced since becoming a Christian. How is your life different? How does Jesus impact your daily life?

Mentally preparing your testimonial story before you are asked by someone is important. Give considerable thought to this, perhaps even writing it down. Here are six things to remember when writing your story:[76]

1. Keep in mind that you are speaking with a pre-Christian.

2. Avoid exclusive language.

3. Avoid exaggeration; the best testimonies are believable.

4. Be clear and concise; it should take about 3 minutes to communicate it.

5. Make the essence of your story what Christ has done for you.

6. Find a Scripture that sums up your story and incorporate it.

Third: His Story

Listening to the story of another person builds relationship and gains a hearing. Sharing your story makes you interesting and relatable. But the power of salvation is found in Jesus' story. Being a good friend or simply sharing your personal conversion story (testimony) is not enough. People need to hear His Story. His Story is "Good News" (Gospel). The Gospel is the Story of Jesus, the story of a hero, a rescuer for humanity. Jesus is the Gospel. Hearing others' stories and telling our own stories are the groundwork laid for telling His Story.

Jesus' story is comprised of four parts (1 Corinthians 15:3-5). Jesus died, he was buried, he was raised, and he appeared to many witnesses. These are the crucial events of His Story. By these events, Jesus' story intersects with our own and become "our story."

1. **Jesus died.** Jesus died for our sins in order to save us.[77] He died "with us" by entering fully into the human condition. He died "instead of us" paying the penalty our sin owes. He died "for us" liberating us from the enslavement of sin and uniting us into the life of God.

2. **Jesus was buried.** Jesus entered fully into human death. Jesus plunges himself headlong into humanity's greatest enemy face-to-face and conquers it for us. His burial sets up the resurrection.

3. **Jesus was raised.** In his bodily resurrection from the dead, Jesus proves his identity as King over all creation (even death itself). He is the "first fruits" of the resurrection (1 Corinthians 15:23), blazing the trail for his followers to also experience life after death.

4. *Jesus appeared.* Jesus appeared in bodily form, not as some disembodied spirit or hovering ghost (Luke 24:39). His bodily appearance is a foreshadowing of the new bodies his followers will inhabit in the new creation (1 Corinthians 15:35-49).

The Bible is God's story. God's story begins with the story of creation, flows into the story of the nation of Israel, is fulfilled in the story of Jesus. The Gospel is the Story of Jesus and how he is the Savior-King of the world.

The first section of this book, called *"Finding Your Place in God's Story,"* is designed to guide you through this Story.

Making Disciples:
Where Do I Start?

Jesus not only had the right message for making disciples, he had the right method.[78]

From Consumer to Missional

How did Jesus launch his disciple-making mission? He did not choose professionals. He chose everyday people, fishermen and accountants (Matthew 4:19; Acts 4:13). But these untrained, uneducated people did something extraordinary. Because of them, Christianity took flight into the ancient world. Jesus came to empower each one of us to know the purpose and mission of being his disciples. He doesn't want any of us to wait around on the supposed "professionals." He wants us to be self-starters who take initiative, take ownership of our faith, and embrace his mission of disciple-making.

The Jesus-Method

Jesus not only had the perfect message, he had the perfect method for making disciples. The church will be renewed when we dedicate ourselves to restoring his method of making disciples. How did he do it?

First, Jesus invested deeply in a few. Occasionally Jesus did teach the crowds. But the world would not be changed by speaking to an amphitheater of listeners. Most of the recorded teachings of Jesus are in private conversations he had with a few of his followers. Jesus chose and invested his life into 12 selected people. Of these, he especially mentored three (Peter, James and John). He modeled life, mentored them, and then sent them out to reproduce the process. Why did Jesus spend so much of his time with so few? He knew deep relationships were the environment to create real disciples.

Second, Jesus created a reproducible process. Jesus' strategy was not one of addition, it was one of multiplication. How did he do this? First, he ministered to others while the disciples watched (Mark 1). Second, he allowed them to assist his ministry (John 6:1-13). At times, the disciples ministered while Jesus assisted them (Mark 9). Finally, he sent them out to minister while he observed (Mark 6:6-12). Jesus hand-selected some teachable people, made them into disciples, trained them for 3 years, then sent them out to do the same thing. His ministry was not focused on the masses; it was built on a select few. *"Disciples are not mass produced but are the product of intimate and personal investment"* in smaller relational contexts. [79] Jesus had enough vision to think small. This approach did not limit his influence; it expanded it. Paul followed this same model (2 Timothy 2:2).

The Discipleship Process

God wants each of us to be progressing down the discipleship path. Where are you in this process? No matter where you are in development, you can be a disciple-maker. Making disciples is not limited to making unbelievers into believers (although such is vital). It also involves helping anyone to move down the process of becoming a more mature disciple.

Growing in our discipleship is pictured in the Bible with many images parallel to the growth cycle of any person. [80] Spiritually, we are "born again" and become infants, then children, grow into young adults, mature into parents and eventually become grandparents. We are each at a different stage in the process, and all of us need someone to come alongside and mentor us (disciple us).

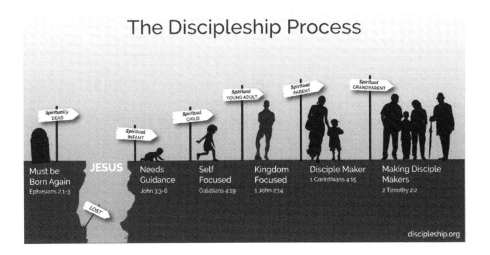

Like plants growing in a greenhouse, the ideal environment for disciple-making is small, relational contexts. These contexts should be characterized by three things:[81]

1. *Vulnerability*- giving permission for the Spirit to more fully enter your life

2. *Discovery of truth*- opening your life to the Spirit's conviction to shape your life

3. *Accountability* –giving others permission to hold you to your commitment

Genuine relationships in small gatherings provide settings of vulnerability, trust, confidentiality, and accountability that accelerate spiritual growth.

Discipleship Groups

A *Discipleship Group (D-Group)* is a gender specific group of 3-5 people who meet together weekly to intentionally pursue accelerated, spiritual growth and learn to disciple others. The group enters into a covenant of honesty, trust, confidentiality, transparency, and accountability with the mutual goal of building up one another and pursuing personal, spiritual growth. The group is highly intentional with a definite roadmap for spiritual growth (see the second section of this book, *Foundations of Discipleship* or *Discipleship Essentials* by Greg Ogden). A *D-Group* is built upon several concepts:

1. **A micro group.** A group of 3-5 people who gather weekly enter a process of accelerated spiritual growth and learn to disciple others. This size is the sweet spot for both transparency/accountability and reproducibility.

2. **A gender-specific group.** To encourage deep sharing and accountability, the groups are gender exclusive.

3. **A group that enters a covenant.** The group enters into a relational commitment to journey together by forming a covenant (i.e. band of brothers; sisterhood pact). (See the Discipleship Group Covenant example on page 254).

4. **Meets weekly for approximately 90 minutes.** Meeting for 90 minutes provides time for personal sharing and exploring the discipleship content.

5. **The group shares mutual ownership.** In a discipleship group, Jesus is the teacher, and we are all his disciples. For this reason, weekly facilitation is rotated among the group.

6. ***A group devoted to deep relationship.*** You will develop deep relationships with others who have the same dedication to spiritual growth.

7. ***A group devoted to spiritual growth.*** Completing this process will accelerate your spiritual growth. You will be spiritually stronger as a result of this group having progressed further down the journey of discipleship.

8. ***A group devoted to mission.*** The process of disciple-making will be modeled, equipping you with a reproducible process that you can replicate with others.

9. ***A group aimed toward replication.*** The group has a definite end date (usually after 12-18 months). From the beginning of the group, each disciple is challenged to consider beginning a new group and replicate the process at the end of the term.

What Makes a D-Group Work?

For a discipling environment to work well, there are three vital components that must be in place.[82]

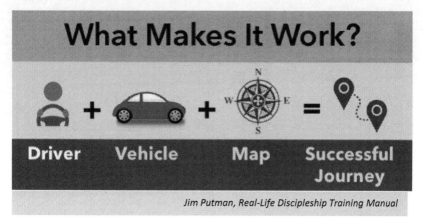

Jim Putman, Real-Life Discipleship Training Manual

1. *A driver (starter)* who intentionally decides to start a group with a clearly stated purpose of discipleship growth.

2. *A vehicle* of discipleship growth is created by cultivating a relational environment.

3. *A map* or clear process (with a study guide or curriculum) of measuring progress and leading others on a journey of discipleship.

How to Start a D-Group

There are four steps that you can take to start your own Discipleship Group (D-Group):

1. ***Begin with prayer*** (Luke 6:12-16). Ask God to send you men or women who have a desire to learn and grow in discipleship (i.e. family members, friends, coworkers, fellow church members, religiously uninvolved, spiritually younger, spiritually older, etc.).

2. ***Look for specific people*** (Luke 10:5-12). Look for people that are:
   - Faithful: show commitment
   - Available: willing to invest
   - Teachable: willing to learn and live the Jesus-life [83]

3. ***Start to recruit*** (2 Timothy 2:2). Invite people into whose lives you can deeply invest.

4. ***Form your group with intentionality*** (Matthew 28:19-20). Pledge to meet regularly together to pursue discipleship growth with the goal to replicate the process.

Discipleship Group Covenant [84]

The discipling process should not begin without every person praying over, and signing a covenant of commitment. Without this agreement, there is no mutually agreed-upon standards of accountability. Accelerated growth in discipleship requires this type of intentionality.

In order to grow toward maturity in Christ, I commit myself to the following expectations:

1. Complete all assignments on a weekly basis prior to my discipleship appointment in order to contribute fully.

2. Meet weekly with my discipleship partners for approximately 90 minutes to dialogue over the content of the assignments (unless providentially hindered).

3. Offer myself fully to the Lord with the anticipation that I am entering a time of accelerated transformation during this discipleship period.

4. Contribute to a climate of honesty, trust, confidentiality, transparency and personal vulnerability in a spirit of mutual up-building.

5. Give serious consideration to continuing the discipling chain (replicating) by committing myself to invest in 2-4 other people for the year following the initial completion of this group.

Signed_____

Dated_____

There will be several opportunities to self-assess and recommit to the covenant. If you are having difficulty keeping the covenant, you will be offered assistance from the group. If inconsistency continues, you might need to consider the timing of the group for your life.

Discipleship Group Guidelines [85]

By Jim Putman

It is vital to creating safe environments where relationships can grow. Implement these guidelines and watch the relationships and transparency of your group grow deeper.

SAFE GROUP: We will strive to create an environment where everyone can be real, open, and honest about our lives. Whether we are feeling discouraged or we are happy, angry or anxious, we should be free to share our real lives.

CONFIDENTIALITY: What is said between us stays between us. This is non-negotiable.

LISTEN: Let's value one another during the discussions by really listening to what is being shared. Try to avoid thinking about how you are going to respond, or what you are going to say next.

PAUSE: Allow a pause in conversation after someone shares. Give the person sharing the chance to finish, and the group the opportunity to consider what was just shared before responding.

SILENCE: It is important to allow silence in the group as it provides an opportunity for someone to share and for members in the group to process the topic or question being considered.

NO DISTRACTIONS: Give your full attention to the person speaking-no phone calls, text messages, or side conversations.

NO FIXING: Sometimes we just need someone to listen. We don't necessarily have to solve each other's problems; we do need to give encouragement, speak truth, and point to Jesus.

NO RESCUING: When people are sharing something deeply personal, there can be a tendency to try to make them feel better about themselves or the situation by providing immediate condolences. This will often cause them to stop sharing. Resist the temptation to rescue people.

SHARING: Be sensitive about the amount of time you share. Don't monopolize your time together-it is important that everyone has a chance to share.

BE SELF-AWARE: Be self-aware of how you are personally affecting the environment through your words, actions and non-verbal communication.

USE "I" STATEMENTS: It's easy to talk about the issues of others, but for our purposes, we want you to put yourself on the table. Try to use "I" statements rather than "them," "us," "we," etc.

RESOLVE CONFLICT: We will commit to resolve conflict biblically. When conflict or sin issues between group members arise, we want to make sure that we are honoring God and each other in the way we deal with these issues. The following are just a few key Scriptures in this regard (there are many others).
- If someone sins against you (Matthew 18:15-20)
- Restoring someone in sin (Galatians 6:1-5)
- Forgive a sinner (Colossians 3:12-13)
- Reconciling differences (Matthew 5:23-24, Matthew 7:1-5)

Recommended Reading on Disciple Making:

Robby Gallaty. *Growing Up: How to Be a Disciple Who Makes Disciples.* (Nashville: B&H, 2013). *This is a great, practical introduction on how to become a disciple-maker.*

Greg Ogden. *Discipleship Essentials.* Expanded Edition. (Downers Grove: Intervarsity, 2007). *This is a recommended curriculum for use in Discipleship Groups of 3-5 people.*

Jim Putman. *Real-Life Discipleship.* (Colorado Springs: NavPress, 2010). *This book provides a roadmap in how to change the culture of a church into disciple-making.*

Jim Putman and Robby Harrington. *Disciple Shift.* (Grand Rapids: Zondervan, 2013). *This book is the definitive resource for making the shift into the mission of disciple-making. This book is a top recommendation.*

Endnotes

[1] Tim Keller. *The Reason for God.* (New York: Riverhead, 2008), 126.

[2] Francis Collins. *The Language of God.* (New York: Free Press, 2006), 102.

[3] *ESV Study Bible*, 2025.

[4] Illustration developed by Timothy Keller and used on several occasions. Cited: 31 May 2016. Online: http://www.scofield.org/2-uncategorised/55-the-story

[5] Randy Frazee. The Heart of the Story. (Grand Rapids, Zondervan, 2011), 9.

[6] Bobette Baxter. *Do/Story/ How to Tell Your Story So the World Listens.* (n.p.: Do Book, 2013), 11.

[7] Brian D. McLaren. *More Ready Than You Realize.* (Grand Rapids: Zondervan, 2006), 113.

[8] McLaren, 113.

[9] Some of these questions are adopted from *The Disciple's Handbook: New Edition.* DPI, 2005.

[10] Randy Frazee. *The Heart of the Story.* (Grand Rapids: Zondervan, 2011), 27.

[11] This exercise is from pages 52-54 of James Bryan Smith's book *The Good and Beautiful God* (IVP: 2009).

[12] Jack Cottrell. *Set Free! What the Bible Says About Grace.* (Joplin: College Press, 2009), 68.

[13] Timothy Keller. *Counterfeit Gods.* (New York: Riverhead, 2009), 89.

[14] This list was adapted from "Basic Bible Studies" from the Dallas/Fort Worth Church of Christ.

[15] Timothy Keller. "The Final Hour." (16 April 2000). Cited: 7 March 2017. Online: http://www.gospelinlife.com/the-final-hour-5188

[16] Jack Cottrell. *The Faith Once for All.* (Joplin, MO: College Press, 2002), 313.

[17] West, Larry. *Getting to the Point…The Gospel Point.* (Fort Worth: Star Bible, 1994), 105.

[18] Timothy Keller. *Songs of Jesus.* (New York: Viking, 2015), xi.

[19] A.W. Tozer. *I Call It Heresy* (Harrisburg, PA: Christian Publications, 1974), 5f.

[20] Dallas Willard. *The Great Omission.* (New York: HarperCollins, 2006), 5.

[21] Dallas Willard. *The Spirit of the Disciplines.* (New York: HarperCollins, 1988), xi.

[22] Patrick Morley. *Seven Seasons of the Man in the Mirror.* (Grand Rapids: Zondervan, 1997), 142.

[23] J.I. Packer. *Knowing God.* (Downers Grove: IVP), 19.

[24] Friedrich Schiller. *Letter 4 Theosophy of Julius.*

[25] Carl Sagan. *The Pale Blue Dot.* (New York: Ballantine, 1994), 6

[26] Packer. *Knowing God.* 75-81.

[27] Packer, *Knowing God.* 21.

[28] I first heard this observation from Timothy Keller.

[29] R. Kent Hughes. *James: Faith That Works.* (Wheaton: Crossway, 1991) 186-7.

[30] Martin Luther. *Commentary on the Epistle to the Galatians* (1535). Theodore Graebner, trans. (Grand Rapids: Zondervan, 1949), 68-85. Cited: 10 Sept. 2018. Online: https://www.iclnet.org/pub/resources/text/wittenberg/luther/gal/web/gal2-17.html

[31] James Bryan Smith. *The Good and Beautiful God.* (Downer's Grove, Illinois: 2009) 90-91.

[32] C.S. Lewis. *Mere Christianity.* (New York: Touchstone, 1996), 9-10.

[33] Alex Koo. "Why Lose Your Life? A New View of Self-Denial." Cited: 22 June 2015. Online: http://alexkooblog.com/why-lose-your-life-a-new-view-on-self-denial/.

[34] John W. Smith. "Holiness and the Holy Spirit." *Angel Fire In-Depth Symposium.* Angel Fire, NM. July 24-27, 2014.

[35] Jan Johnson. "Dying to Self and Discovering So Much More" Cited: 17 Nov. 2015. Online: http://billygraham.org/decision-magazine/september-2011/dying-to-self-and-discovering-so-much-more/comment-page-6/

[36] Francis Chan. *Basic. Follow Jesus*. Video. (Grand Rapids: Flannel, 2010).

[37] Much of this lesson is adapted from: Gordon MacDonald. *Ordering Your Private World*. (Nashville: Thomas Nelson, 1984).

[38] "Heart." *Nelson's New Illustrated Bible Dictionary*. Ronald F. Youngblood, ed. (Nashville: Thomas Nelson, 1995), 548-9.

[39] William R. Moody. *D.L. Moody*. (1930), chapter 66, p. 503.

[40] Timothy Keller. Timothy Keller@TimKellerNYC. Facebook post. July 24, 2015.

[41] Wayne Cordeiro. *Leading on Empty*. (Minneapolis: Bethany House, 2009), 78-9.

[42] Wayne Cordeiro. *Leading On Empty*. (Minneapolis: Bethany, 2009), 88.

[43] James Bryan Smith. *The Good and Beautiful God*. (Downers Grove: InterVarsity, 2009), 33.

[44] Smith, 130.

[45] Smith, 130.

[46] Rick Warren. *The Purpose Driven Life*. (Grand Rapids: Zondervan, 2002), 190.

[47] Much of this lesson is adapted from: Andy Stanley. "Permission to Speak Freely" sermon series. https://store.northpoint.org/products/permission-to-speak-freely-audio-download

[48] Francis Chan. "Prayer is a Way of Walking in Love." Cited: 15 Dec. 2015. Online: https://www.youtube.com/watch?v=yzokhJ_3G-4

[49] Daniel Henderson. *Transforming Prayer*. (Minneapolis: Bethany House, 2011), 27.

[50] Much of this lesson is adapted from: Andy Stanley. "Permission to Speak Freely" sermon series. https://store.northpoint.org/products/permission-to-speak-freely-audio-download

[51] Daniel Henderson. *Transforming Prayer*. (Minneapolis, Minnesota: Bethany House, 2011), 27.

[52] Timothy Keller. "Preaching in a Post-Modern Climate." Cited: 30 Oct 2015. Online: http://storage.cloversites.com/citychurch/documents/Preaching%20the%20Gospel%20in%20a%20Post%20Modern%20Culture.pdf.

[53] Jack Cottrell. "Saved by Grace #6—Grace vs. Galatianism." Cited: 3 Nov. 2011. Online: http://jackcottrell.com/uncategorized/saved-by-grace-6-grace-vs-galatianism/

[54] Jack Cottrell, "Saved by Grace #6"

[55] Timothy Keller, "Preaching in a Post-Modern Climate."

[56] Timothy Keller. *Counterfeit Gods.* (New York: Riverhead, 2009), 168.

[57] John Ortberg. *God is Closer Than You Think.* (Grand Rapids: Zondervan, 2005), 27.

[58] Jon Hamilton. "Einstein's Brain Unlocks Some Mysteries of the Mind." Cited: 6 Nov. 2015. Online: http://www.npr.org/templates/story/story.php?storyId=126229305.

[59] Martin Luther. *Treatise on Good Works.* Cited: 4 December 2015. Online: http://www.gutenberg.org/files/418/418-h/418-h.htm.

[60] Timothy Keller. *Counterfeit Gods.* (New York: Riverhead, 2009), xix.

[61] J.I. Packer. "Killing Sin Through Personal Prayer." Cited: 18 August 2015. Online: http://www.desiringgod.org/articles/killing-sin-through-personal-prayer.

[62] John Owen. *Overcoming Sin and Temptation.* Kelly Kapic and Justin Taylor, eds. (Wheaton: Crossway, 2006), 30.

[63] Timothy Keller. "Peace." Cited: 3 December 2015. Online: https://www.youtube.com/watch?v=cajScztdhJA.

[64] Dallas Willard. *Renovation of the Heart* (Colorado Springs: NavPress, 2002), 101-2.

[65] Timothy Keller. "The Marks of the Spirit." Cited: 4 December 2015. Online: http://www.gospelinlife.com/the-marks-of-the-spirit-5665. These two steps are seen in numerous passages like Romans 8; Colossians 3; Hebrews 12.

[66] John Owen. *Overcoming Sin and Temptation.* 49-57.

[67] Andy Stanley. "Communication: How to Give a Talk." Cited: 4 December 2015. Online: https://www.youtube.com/watch?v=9GSVSfaCyf8

[68] J.I. Packer. *Knowing God.* 23.

[69] Stanley. "Communication."

[70] Timothy Keller. "All of Life is Repentance." Cited: 10 December 2015. Online: http://crupressgreen.com/all-of-life-is-repentance/

[71] Timothy Keller. "Neighbors." Cited 5 March 2015. Online: http://sermons2.redeemer.com/sermons/neighbors.

[72] Tim Mackie. "How to Read the Bible." Cited: 6 Sept. 2019. Online: https://thebibleproject.com/explore/how-to-read-the-bible/

[73] Suggestions 1-5 are adapted from: Brian McLaren. *More Ready Than You Realize.* (Grand Rapids: Zondervan, 2006), 14-50. Suggestions 9-14 are adapted from: Joshua D. Chatraw and Mark D. Allen. *Apologetics at the Cross.* (Grand Rapids: Zondervan, 2018), 163-167.

[74] Dallas Willard. *The Allure of Gentleness.* (New York: Harper Collins, 2016), 49.

[75] The insights for crafting a personal testimony are adapted from: "Postmodern Evangelism Training." Cited: 6 Sept. 2019. Online: https://media.tlc.org/ministries/ college/downloads/PostmodernEvangelism.pdf

[76] "Postmodern Evangelism Training." Cited: 6 Sept. 2019. Online: https:// media.tlc.org/ministries/college/downloads/PostmodernEvangelism.pdf

[77] This three-fold benefit of Jesus' death is from: Scot McKnight. *The King Jesus Gospel.* (Grand Rapids: Zondervan, 2016) 51-52.

[78] David M. Young. *New Day: Restoring the Revolutionary Mission of Christ's Church.* (Murfreesboro, TN: New Day Press, 2016), 149.

[79] Greg Ogden. *Discipleship Essentials.* (Downers Grove: Intervarsity, 2007), 20.

[80] Jim Putman & Bobby Harrington. *Discipleshift.* (Grand Rapids: Zondervan, 2013).

[81] Greg Ogden, *Discipleship Essentials.* 15.

[82] Jim Putman. *Real-Life Discipleship Training Manual.* (Colorado Springs: NavPress, 2010), 60

[83] Robby Gallaty. *Growing Up: How to Be a Disciple Who Makes Disciples.* (Nashville: B&H, 2013), 181-182.

[84] This covenant is adapted from Greg Odgen's excellent resource: Greg Ogden. *Discipleship Essentials.* (Downer's Grove: Intervarsity, 1998), 14.

[85] Jim Putman. "12 Guidelines for Small Group Discussions." Cited: 18 Sept. 2019. Online: https://jimputman.com/2018/10/01/are-you-missing-these-12-effective-small-group-discussion-guidelines/

Made in the USA
Columbia, SC
18 January 2023

75491427R00143